THE
NEW
WORLD

A BOOK OF THE
NEW MESSAGE
FROM GOD

THE
NEW
WORLD

THE FUTURE
of
HUMANITY

AS REVEALED TO

Marshall Vian Summers

THE
NEW
WORLD

Edited by Darlene Mitchell
Cover and interior: Designed by Reed Summers

ISBN: 978-1-942293-46-0 (POD)
ISBN: 978-1-942293-47-7 (ebook)
NKL POD Version 7.05 ; Sv7.3 6/12/19
Library of Congress Control Number: 2019940433

Publisher's Cataloging-in-Publication Data
(Prepared by The Donohue Group, Inc.)

Names: Summers, Marshall Vian, author. | Society for the New Message.
Title: The new world : the future of humanity / as revealed to Marshall
    Vian Summers.
Description: Boulder, CO : New Knowledge Library, the publishing imprint
    of The Society for the New Message, [2019] | Series: The New Message
    from God. [Volume 1, book 7]
Identifiers: ISBN 9781942293460 (POD) | ISBN 9781942293477 (ebook)
Subjects: LCSH: Society for the New Message--Doctrines. | Environmental
    degradation--Religious aspects. | Religion and social problems.
    | Spiritual Life. | Mystical union.
Classification: LCC BP605.S58 S863 2019 (print) | LCC BP605.S58 (ebook)
    | DDC 299/.93--dc23

The New World is a book of the New Message from God and is published by New Knowledge Library, the publishing imprint of The Society for the New Message. The Society is a religious non-profit organization dedicated to presenting and teaching a New Message for humanity. The books of New Knowledge Library can be ordered at www.newknowledgelibrary.org, your local bookstore and at many other online retailers.

The New Message is being studied in more than 30 languages in over 90 countries. *The New World* is being translated into the many languages of our world by a dedicated group of volunteer student translators from around the world. These translations will all be available online at www.newmessage.org.

The Society for the New Message
P.O. Box 1724   Boulder, CO 80306-1724
(303) 938-8401   (800) 938-3891
011 303 938 84 01 (International)   (303) 938-1214 (fax)
newmessage.org   newknowledgelibrary.org
email: society@newmessage.org

*W*e shall speak of God, the Higher Authority.

———————

*T*he Higher Authority is speaking to you now, speaking through the Angelic Presence, speaking to a part of you that is the very center and source of your Being.

———————

*T*he Higher Authority has a Message for the world, and for each person in the world.

———————

*T*he Higher Authority is calling to you, calling to you down through the Ancient Corridors of your mind, calling to you beyond your beliefs and your preoccupations.

———————

*F*or God has spoken again and the Word and the Sound are in the world.

From *God Has Spoken Again,*
Chapter 3: The Engagement

THE
NEW
WORLD

TABLE OF CONTENTS

INTRODUCTION

The New World is a book of Revelation given by the Creator of all life to the human family through the Messenger Marshall Vian Summers.

Throughout history, God has given Revelation and Wisdom to meet the growing needs of our world at great turning points in the evolution of humanity. Now God is speaking again, delivering a New Revelation to meet the critical needs of humanity as it faces Great Waves of environmental, political and economic change and contact with a Greater Community of intelligent life in the universe.

God's progressive Revelation is continuing anew through a New Message from God, of which *The New World* is but a part. The words of this text are a direct communication from the Creator of all life, translated into human language by the Angelic Presence that watches over this world, and then spoken through the Messenger Marshall Vian Summers, who has given over 30 years of his life to this process of Revelation.

The New Message from God is an original communication from God to the heart of every person on Earth. It is not for one nation, one tribe or one religion alone. It is a Message for the entire world, a world facing very different needs and challenges from those of ancient times.

This communication is here to ignite the spiritual power of humanity, to sound God's calling for unity amongst the world's nations and religions, and to prepare humanity for a radically changing world and for its destiny in a larger universe of intelligent life.

The New Message from God speaks on nearly every aspect of life facing people today. It is the largest Revelation ever given to humanity, given now to a literate world of global communication and growing global awareness. Never before has there been a

Divine Revelation of this size, given by God to all people of the world at once, in the lifetime of the Messenger.

Yet the New Message from God has not entered the world through the existing religious authorities and institutions of today. It has not come to the leaders of religion or to those who garner fame and recognition. Instead, it has been given to a humble man chosen and sent into the world for this one task, to be a Messenger for this New Message for humanity.

The Messenger has walked a long and difficult road to bring the New Message from God to you and to the world. The process of Revelation began in 1982 and continues to this day. The Messenger's story is one of perseverance, humility and lifelong service to others. His presence in the world today represents an opportunity to know him and receive the Revelation directly from him.

At the center of the New Message is the original Voice of Revelation, which has spoken the words of every book of the New Message. Never before has the Voice of Revelation, the Voice that spoke to the Messengers and prophets of the past, been recorded in its original purity and made available to each person to hear and to experience for themselves. In this way, the Word and the Sound of God's Revelation are in the world.

In this remarkable process of spoken Revelation, the Presence of God communicates beyond words to the Angelic Assembly that oversees the world. The Assembly then translates this communication into human language and speaks all as one through their Messenger, whose voice becomes the vehicle for this greater Voice—the Voice of Revelation.

The words of this Voice have been recorded in audio form, transcribed and are now available in the books of the New Message. In addition, the original audio recordings of the Voice of Revelation are available for all to hear. In this way, the purity of God's original spoken Message is preserved and given to all people in the world.

At this time, the Messenger is engaged in compiling over three decades of spoken Revelation into a final and complete text—The One Book of the New Message from God. This book of Revelation will ultimately be divided into six volumes and possibly more. Each volume will contain two or more books, and each book will be organized by chapter and verse. Therefore, the New Message from God will be structured in the following way: Volume > Book > Chapter > Verse.

The New World is the seventh book of Volume 1 of the New Message from God and The New World contains 16 individual revelations (chapters) revealed to the Messenger at different times. The Messenger has compiled these revelations into the text you see today.

In order to bring this spoken communication into written form, slight textual and grammatical adjustments were made by the Messenger. This was requested of him by the Angelic Assembly to aid the understanding of the reader and to convey the Message according to the grammatical standards of the written English language.

In some instances, the Messenger has inserted a word not originally spoken in the Revelation. When present, you will often find this inserted word in brackets. Consider these bracketed words as direct clarifications by the Messenger, placed in the text by him alone in order to ensure that ambiguities in the spoken communication do not cause confusion or incorrect interpretations of the text.

In some cases, the Messenger has removed a word to aid the readability of the text. This was usually done in the case of certain conjunctions (words such as *and*, *but*) that made the text unnecessarily awkward or grammatically incorrect.

The Messenger alone has made these slight changes and only to convey the original spoken communication with the greatest clarity possible. None of the original meaning or intention of the communication has been altered.

The text of this book has been structured by the Messenger into verse. Each verse roughly signals the beginning or ending of a distinct message point communicated by the Source.

The verse structure of the text allows the reader to access the richness of the content and those subtle messages that may otherwise be missed in longer paragraphs of text that convey multiple topics. In this way, each topic and idea communicated by the Source is given its own standing, allowing it to speak from the page directly to the reader. The Messenger has determined that structuring the text in verse is the most efficacious and faithful way of rendering the original spoken revelations of the New Message.

Through this text, we are witnessing the process of preparation and compilation being undertaken by the Messenger, in his own time, by his own hands. This stands in stark contrast to the fact that the former great traditions were rarely put into written form by their Messengers, leaving the original messages vulnerable to alteration and corruption over time.

Here the Messenger seals in purity the texts of God's New Message and gives them to you, to the world and to all people in the future. Whether this book is opened today or 500 years from now, God's original communication will speak from these pages with the same intimacy, purity and power as it did the day it was first spoken.

Though it appears to be a book in the hand, *The New World* is something far greater. It is a calling and a communication from the Heart of God to you. In the pages of this book, God's Presence calls to you and to all people, calling for you to awaken from the dream and nightmare of living in Separation apart from your Source, calling to the presence of "Knowledge," the deeper spiritual Intelligence that lives within you, waiting to be discovered.

The New World is part of a living communication from God to humanity. Remarkably, you have found the New Message from God, or it has found you. It is no coincidence that this is the case. This opens the next chapter in the mystery of your life and of your presence in the world at this time. The door opens before you. You need only enter to begin.

As you enter more deeply into the Revelation, the impact on your life will grow, bringing a greater experience of clarity, inner certainty and true direction to your life. In time, your questions will be answered as you find growing freedom from self-doubt, inner conflict and the restraints of the past. Here the Creator of all life is speaking to you directly, revealing to you the greater life that you were always destined to live.

The Society for the New Message from God

CHAPTER 1

ENTERING THE NEW WORLD

As revealed to
Marshall Vian Summers
on April 4, 2011
in Boulder, Colorado

You are preparing for a new world, a world that has already changed, a world that has been changed by human ignorance, abuse and neglect. You passed the line some time ago, where the world changed imperceptibly, an unknown marker in the evolution of humanity.

Now you are in a new world—a world unlike the world you are accustomed to, a world with a changing and different climate, a world with diminishing resources, a world of polluted and contaminated rivers and soils, a world where ever-growing numbers of people will be drinking from a slowly shrinking well.

This is the new world. It has changed already. But people have not changed. Perhaps you have not really changed, except in superficial ways. People do not know they are living in a different world—a new world, a world that will be much more disorderly, a world where nature will change the terms of engagement in subtle and dramatic ways, a world that could have been foreseen and has been foreseen by certain prescient individuals, a world for which humanity is sadly unprepared and still does not recognize.

Except in times of great natural disaster and calamity, people rarely recognize how much nature is allowing them to live, how the stability of the world and its climate and living conditions physically, fundamentally, have enabled human civilization to grow and to expand. People have lost their connection with the natural world, and so they have become ignorant of its greater hazards, and have lost appreciation for the great benefits it has provided to the human family through its long period of great stability.

In the new world, you will not have this stability. It has changed. And the demonstration that it has changed is now appearing here and there, in this country and that country, and then in another country—as if everything were speeding up, as if events that only occurred very infrequently are now occurring frequently in many places. This is part of the new world.

God is here to prepare you for the new world. We are here to prepare you for the new world. The preparation is very significant, but it requires a tremendous reconsideration of so many things that perhaps you individually have never thought of before, or have ever concerned yourself with—such as where your food and water come from, the degree to which they may be contaminated and the degree to which their delivery to you can be disrupted and likely will be disrupted in the times to come.

If you can respond to this clearly, you will see that it is the fundamental elements of life that are of the greatest significance. The machinations of politics and culture, the trends of society become far less significant in the light of these things.

In the new world, food, water and energy will become ever more predominating, ever more the priority for the stability of nations and communities within nations.

The transition is difficult because people are still living in the past, living on a set of assumptions that they have never had to question significantly unless they were faced with natural calamities on a great scale.

In times of calamity, people wake up briefly and then slowly go back to sleep. "That was a terrible thing that happened, years ago. We remember it. But now we are going back to sleep. It won't happen again for centuries, so we are going back to sleep"—lulled to sleep by human complacency, human denial, human preoccupation, human distractions, by all the forces of society that want to lull you into becoming a manageable consumer, the rules of religion that specify how life and God should be considered, the preoccupations of a nation in its relations with other nations—going back into old routines, forgetting about the past, [thinking] it is over.

Humanity will have to be ever more vigilant in the new world, ever more careful, ever more considering of the consequences of current actions, more restrained in its use of resources, more restrained in how nations intervene with one another, more circumspect, more responsible, more concerned with the outcome in the future.

Already a large proportion of humanity is hungry, does not have clean water, does not have stability and security in their own villages, towns and communities. This will grow, leading nations into revolution, bringing into power even more dangerous individuals and groups, creating further instability. Even the average citizen now must begin to wake up from their obsessions, their addictions and their preoccupations in order to pay attention to the changing circumstances of life around them.

It is this time which can be so redeeming, so clarifying, so sobering, bringing people into the present, where they can seek more simple pleasures, more natural activities and become more present to one another, more available to one another, more comprehending of what they see around them.

It is within this [time] that certain individuals will begin to reclaim a greater Intelligence that resides within each person—an Intelligence which We call Knowledge—a greater Mind unspoiled by the world, unafraid of the world, here on a greater mission that is your mission, accountable only to God and to the great Angelic Presence that serves the Creator in this world and throughout the universe.

This is a time of great shock and dismay, but it is also a time of great clarification, a time when your true calling will emerge from the world, for you cannot call yourself. Your gifts are meant to be given in certain places, to certain people, and this is rarely reflected in people's goals and aspirations. As the world grows more dark, more problematic, more unstable, more disconcerting, the calling will be stronger, more powerful, more engaging for those who can respond.

In affluence, human complacency increases. Human indulgence increases. Human addiction increases. Human pathology increases. Mental illness increases—strangely enough. In this, the rich can be more pathetic than the poor. In this, the wealthy nations can squander their freedom, their natural inheritance, their environment, their resources, their time, their energy and their creativity—lost, gone, gone forever, spent unwisely.

This is the tragedy of living in the world without Knowledge. It is the tragedy in every person's life, for everyone was sent here for a greater purpose and everyone was given Knowledge to guide them to this purpose and to prepare them for this purpose.

But the majority of people in the world are oppressed—oppressed by political oppression; oppressed by poverty; oppressed by social and religious dictates; oppressed because they have no social power and no mobility; they cannot change their circumstances—a great loss for the human family as a whole, as a majority of the great scientists, the great physicians, the great social emancipators, the great artists, the great musicians are lost, oppressed, their gifts never to be seen, their lives wasted.

In the new world, the tragedy of the common person will become so acute and so demanding that many people who are not responding today will have to respond. Whole nations of people will not be able to sustain themselves. Even the wealthy nations will not have the resources to provide endless welfare for nations that are unstable or impoverished. This will be a calling for individuals and for nations to respond and to prepare.

Humanity lives for the moment. It is careless with its future. It is unwise in its activities and behavior.

War is no longer an option, you see, for it destroys people and the infrastructure and the resources that will be needed for the future. In the new world, this becomes ever more significant.

In the new world, you will have to contend with erratic forces of nature, with an unstable climate and its impact upon the production of food, the diminishing of critical resources and how this will affect the transportation and the growing of food and the purification of water. Your problems will be more elemental, more fundamental and more profound.

The new world can wake you up, but it can also destroy you. That is why you must gain access to the deeper Intelligence within you, the power and the presence of Knowledge that God has given you to navigate this new world and to bring forth your true gifts that still remain hidden within you and others.

In the new world, cooperation will become ever more essential—to save the lives of people, to meet ever-increasing emergencies, to respond to the changing environment and the changing conditions of life. Here the rich must give, or they risk losing everything. Here the poor must be served and must unite to create greater stability beyond the boundaries of culture and religion. For in war and conflict—the kind of war the new world could create—everyone will suffer, everyone will lose.

Regions of the world will become uninhabitable. The problems that will arise will seem so great that they will appear to be insurmountable, and this is why human ingenuity will have to be exercised now in the most constructive ways.

It is pointless for nations to arm themselves to the extreme, for war cannot be an option, or the world will decline, and the future of humanity will be sacrificed.

Every nation will be dependent on the stability of nations around it. It will be in their interest to support this stability within their region of the world. Nations cannot be sacrificed, or tens of millions of people will stream across your borders, creating further instability and far greater difficulty for everyone involved.

Only God knows what is coming over the horizon. God has sent the preparation, the warning, the blessing, the power, the illumination and the clarification. But God does not answer every question, every dilemma and every problem. That, the people of the world must figure out.

You cannot be passive in these matters. You cannot be fooling around in the face of the Great Waves of change. You cannot be idle and indolent in the new world. You must be strong. You must be determined. And you must be compassionate. It is not an environment for the weak and the indulgent. Yet weakness and indulgence is prevalent, especially in the wealthy nations.

Young people have no idea what they are going to have to deal with in the future. Their future has been spent and squandered. They are going to have to face and adapt to a new world. You cannot be idle and complaining and do this. It is not enough to simply be in complaint or revolution. You must think about how things are going to work—practically, essentially, fundamentally.

This is a time when humanity has to grow up, cease its endless conflicts and set aside its foolish indulgences to deal with a changing world, to deal with a new world, to deal with a world their ancestors rarely ever had to contend with, to face a new and rising set of circumstances that will challenge the intention, the integrity and the will to live.

It will be a shock to so many people. Many people will not be able to respond. They have not built the strength in their lives to face a new world. They will be vulnerable. They will be threatened.

If you are to serve the weak, you must have strong allies. You must have the Revelation, or you too will still be submersed in your listless understanding of the past, still caught up in your grievances, still thinking in the old world that no longer exists.

Only God knows what is coming over the horizon. Human speculation rarely accounts for reality. Only those minds that are clear and sober and objective can really see much of anything. Even here their estimation can fall far short of the reality that is emerging and what must be done to prepare for eventualities.

You must look to your life and circumstances. Is your employment going to be able to survive a world where many people will not be able to afford luxuries and discretionary spending? Are you surrounded by people who are weak or strong, people who can respond or people who are lost—lost in their wishes, their fears, their problems, their issues, their complaints, their obsessions and so forth?

You must move to higher ground, mentally and physically. Do not live near the moving waters of the world. Consider the safety and stability of your community. Live near where food is produced, and learn to produce it yourself if you can. Be very careful with your health, for you will need to be very strong and competent in the future. Educate others patiently. Seek those who are able to respond, and do not waste yourself on those who cannot hear and cannot see.

Begin to build a stronger life, a more stable life. The New Revelation will teach you how to do this in the Four Pillars of your life—the Pillar of Relationships, the Pillar of Work and Providership, the Pillar of Health and the Pillar of Spiritual Development.

Everything We tell you is supported by the Revelation. But you cannot simply be passive and think that every little thing will be given to you and shown to you. You will have to become intelligent and use the power of Knowledge and develop your skills, your discernment and your discretion. You cannot be sloppy and foolish now, for everything you say and do is important.

Because you were sent into the world for a greater purpose, you have a greater set of responsibilities to develop. You have to counteract your own laziness, your weakness, your inclination to quit and give up, the amount of fear that you carry and the influence of that fear upon you. It is a great and demanding situation—perfect for your redemption.

If humanity cannot unite in its times of affluence and stability, then it must unite in its times of greater trial and tribulation.

Do not worry what other people are doing. You must be concerned with your own affairs and relationships. But do watch your environment and learn to listen for the signs of change. For this, you will need a still and focused mind, a mind that is not caught up in grievances, fear or ambition. The Revelation will teach you how to cultivate this greater and more penetrating awareness.

Most of the preparation will be internal. For it is what guides your decisions, what guides your actions, what informs you, what motivates you and what discourages you that will make the greater difference in what you will be able to see, to know and to do.

Do not run away and try to hide somewhere, for that will not be successful in the new world. Do not think only of defending yourself, for you are not here in the world to do that, and that will only make you more vulnerable in the end.

You have to shore up your foundation, but beyond that you are here to be of greater service. Knowledge will guide you in this direction. Fear will take you somewhere else. And fear will only bring you into greater jeopardy in the future, should you continue to respond to it alone.

The Messenger is in the world. The Revelation is here. It brings with it its own counsel and commentary. It is not here to give you great commands, but to tell you how to respond, to address the problems and questions that will surely arise and to provide the Steps to Knowledge that will give you the essential grounding and connection to the source and center of your strength, your wisdom and your power.

The new world will be so demanding and so disconcerting. To the weak it will seem overwhelming, and they will feel helpless and hopeless in the face of it.

But you cannot respond like this, for the changing circumstances and the rising tides and the Great Waves of change are here to tell you that you must become stronger, smarter and more responsive to your environment and to the power and presence of Knowledge within you. This will do more to provide you stability and security than anything you try to build on the outside. You cannot stockpile food for the rest of your life. If you hoard things, people can come and steal it from you, even using force.

The New Message is calling you to respond and to prepare. It is not enough to live in the moment only. That is fine for the birds and the beasts and the simple creatures of life, yet they do not have the burden of knowing of their future demise, or caring about their future particularly.

For human beings, living in the moment alone is a demonstration of profound ignorance and the neglect of one's greater Intelligence and responsibilities. In the moment, you can see, hear, and know—but you are always preparing for the future. You are always watching the winds of the world.

If you give up all possessions and become an ascetic, you have fewer concerns, but your role is still here to serve the changing world. And becoming an ascetic is not what is asked for or necessary for most people.

The decisions are before you today. The deep evaluation is before you today—about who you are with and what you are doing, what should be maintained and what should be set aside, what should be changed and what should be preserved, who to be with, who not to be with, what to say, what not to say, what to do, what not to do. That is your stage of development.

You cannot move into the future and try to decide. You are not ready for the future. Therefore, getting ready is all important. It will make all the difference in the outcome for you and for others, for the people you love and for the people you are meant to serve ultimately.

You cannot change the new world. You cannot stop it from being what it is. You can mitigate the errors that humanity continues to make regarding its contamination of the world, and this must be done, of course. But you cannot wish the new world away, and to deny this is merely an act of foolishness and self-denial.

Therefore, you must respond. Look and listen. Do not come to premature conclusions. Face your own fear, but do not succumb to it. Face your own sense of insecurity, but do not succumb to it. Face the fact that you have very few answers for anything, but do not succumb to this either.

You are a student of Knowledge now. You are here to prepare. You are responding to the New Revelation, which will prepare you and teach you how to follow that which is wise within yourself and within other people.

You are blessed to receive this, but the blessing requires a lot of work, patience and determination—qualities that you can only develop by building them and applying them to the real situations of your life. The power and the presence will be with you as you do this.

It is about being honest with yourself, true to your deeper inclinations—not just allegiant to your thoughts or your feelings in the moment, but allegiance to a greater sense and awareness within yourself that is waiting to be discovered and expressed in your life.

Hear Our words. They carry the great Wisdom with them. Listen. Do not deny them. Pay attention. Think of them within the circumstances of your life. Contemplate them. Live with them. Better to live with great questions than to build your life on foolish answers.

God has spoken again—to awaken the world, to prepare the world, to strengthen the human family, to bring forth its greatest assets so that it may utilize the wisdom of its religions, the wisdom of its cultures and the many successes that humanity has achieved in the building of a world civilization.

Everything will be challenged now. Do not think that the good will prevail. Do not use this as an excuse to shrink from your responsibilities. Do not ask God to save the world, for God has sent you and others into the world to save the world. You do not know how to do this, really, if you are honest and humble within yourself. It is a matter for Knowledge to guide you step by step.

For this, you will have to live without answers. You will have to give up your weak assumptions and become close to life, close to the moment, where you discern what is coming over the horizon.

CHAPTER 2

THE GREAT WARNING

As revealed to
Marshall Vian Summers
on April 26, 2015
in Boulder, Colorado

God has sent the New Message to the world at a great turning point for the human family—a turning point for which you are unprepared and unaware, a turning point that is so great that it will alter the course of life for everyone here today, and the future of everyone to come in this world.

It is a great threshold, the greatest the human family has ever had to face, in part due to its despoiling the world and in part due to its evolution, which has brought it to the threshold of space, a Greater Community of life in the universe of which you know nothing at all.

The great Revelations of the past and the Messengers who have brought them here did not prepare you for this, for that was not the need at that time.

But you have now reached the threshold where you are changing the world so sufficiently that it will create an environment that will be ever more difficult for you to survive within. And you are facing Intervention from the universe around you, from those races who seek to exploit your weakness and division and your changing circumstances for their own purposes and benefit.

All the while, humanity is consumed with its own internal problems and its friction between nations, cultures and religions. Consumed it is, self-possessed it is, blind and foolish as it stands at the threshold of the Greater Community, unprepared to deal with the outcome and the effects of its plundering this world to such an extent that it is changing the atmosphere and the waters and the soils—all the very things you depend upon each moment and day to live in this world, this splendid world, a real gem in the universe.

Wrecking the planet has brought others here to save it for themselves, to become the new leadership for this world, if the opportunity can be given to them.

Many people feel great anxiety about the future and concern over what will come, and that is well founded. No matter what explanations they give to this, or what they think it means, it is all the same response to a great change in your circumstances and a great challenge to your freedom and well-being.

Only the Lord of the universe can warn you of these things with perfect clarity. And that is being done now through the Angelic Assembly, who speaks as one Voice to bring God's New Revelation into the world.

For God has not spoken to the world in 1400 years. Messages have come for specific things, through certain agents, but nothing for the whole world, nothing to alter the course of humanity's reckless behavior and destiny.

Revelations of this nature only come perhaps once in a millennium. You are so privileged and challenged to be living at such a time of Revelation. It is the greatest opportunity if you can understand it, if you can receive what God wants to give to humanity, and not just use it for your own selfish purposes, but to bring it to bear on the well-being and the future of the human family in this world, which is now imperiled from within and from without.

For you have changed the chemistry of the atmosphere so sufficiently that the planet will become hotter and the waters will rise. The oceans will rise and they will continue to rise, consuming everything in their wake. Great droughts and storms will lash upon the world as they are beginning to do now.

It will be a time of increasing difficulty and emergency. Do not be surprised that this is occurring, for you have changed the conditions of life here so sufficiently that this could be foreseen and has been foreseen by certain individuals.

But the picture is bigger than this, you see, for your growing vulnerability has brought Intervention from the universe, from exploitive races who may present themselves as being peace loving and in service to humanity. But this is only a deception.

This planet is of great value in the universe. But no one will attack it, for that is not allowed in this part of space. No one wants to destroy its great assets. And no one wants to destroy humanity as its resident work force.

With each passing day, you are losing your self-sufficiency, making you ever vulnerable to persuasion from beyond and inducements from beyond and the offering of gifts from beyond. As humanity's condition continues to decline, who amongst you or your leaders will have the wisdom and the restraint to hold back from receiving these things?

The world is changing so fast, and some of it you cannot change. You can only mitigate it, which is rarely being done in the world today.

For people do not realize they are living in a global state of emergency, the early stages of this where much can be done, where much can be resolved, where much preparation can be underway.

But who amongst those you know, who amongst your culture and nation and family are preparing for the Great Waves of change? Are you preparing for the Great Waves of change? Or are you foolishly living in the moment, blind and ignorant to where you are going and what is coming over the horizon and the great signs the world is giving you now to alert you and to prepare you?

God has given now the preparation for the great change that is coming—given at a time of utmost importance and expediency, given at a time when humanity still has time to prepare and to offset much of the damage that may be done in the future, should you neglect your duties and responsibilities now.

Only God knows what is coming over the horizon. You are concerned with your needs and issues, your grievances and your debates. But you are not even looking. Who amongst anyone you know is really looking? People are hiding behind their religions, their scriptures, people are hiding behind their politics, people are hiding behind their problems. Who has the courage and the humility to look out and to ask in all honesty, "What is coming now?"

People do not want to know. They do not want to see. They do not want to face the challenge, even though facing it will make them stronger than they are today and will give them a chance to do something intelligent for themselves and their loved ones.

Do not seek comfort. Do not seek reprieve. Do not try to find peace and equanimity in a world that you have been sent to serve—a world now facing its greatest challenges and its greatest opportunity for unity and cooperation, if enough people can recognize the great need of this time and the times to come.

It does not matter if you pray to God. It does not matter that you prostrate yourself in the church, the temple or the mosque if you are not willing to really do what God has sent you here to do, which is to play your small but important part in preparing yourself and your nation for the two great challenges that humanity is now facing and will face increasingly as time continues.

There is no greater problem than this. For if you should fail in either of these challenges—if you should fail to prepare for the Great Waves of change; if you should fail to offset the Intervention that is occurring in the world today, which you have the power to do— then human freedom will be lost, and you will be placed in a set of circumstances more difficult and challenging than you can now imagine.

This is such a great challenge and so important that God has spoken again, to address it directly, to prepare you, to bring purpose and equanimity and cooperation between the world's religions, which must all now help to prepare humanity for the great change that is coming. There should be no conflict between them, for God has initiated them all. Though they have all been changed by man over time, they still have great purpose to their Source and service to give to the world in cooperation with one another.

Now you must begin to think of things you have not thought of before, to consider the outcome and the consequences of great events in the world and not merely think about your own personal interests, needs or distractions.

You must become responsible—able to respond, willing to look, recognizing your limitations in doing so, recognizing your weaknesses and your strengths, A deep evaluation for your life must be undertaken at such a time, or the Great Waves will consume you and all that you have. And when it occurs, you will recognize you did not see it coming because you were never looking or paying attention.

The seas will rise. Within the next century and a half, they will rise over a hundred feet. Where are you going to live? What will happen to your ports and cities and your prime farmland? What will happen to the deltas of the world and the millions who live there? Who will take them in when they must flee their nation, unable to survive there any longer? It is this you must consider.

Look at a map of the world and see what will be lost. The majority of the major cities of the world will be flooded and will not be able to be protected. What will happen to all the people who must leave, even [in] the wealthy nations and their cities and their coastlines? Where will they go? What will they do, they, along with you and your recent ancestors, who have changed the climate of the world? As the icecaps melt, as the glaciers melt, as water becomes ever more precious and drought grows worldwide, these are the things that must be mitigated now while you still have a chance to do so. Do not think there are other problems that are more significant than this. Do not discount this.

You must build your ark—for yourself and your family and your community—not for your own needs, but for the needs of everyone around you. If you wait too long, it will be too late to prepare, and everyone will be panicking. All those who would not see and could not see or were too weak or elderly or infirm to prepare—it will be a great panic, a growing panic, a panic between nations, a panic within nations.

We must tell you these things so that you will understand the importance of God's New Revelation for the world and the importance of your being in the world at this time, which is not merely to lose yourself in hobbies, fantasies and personal goals. You have a responsibility to those who sent you and to those who went to great effort to bring you here at this time, under these circumstances, to serve a world facing its greatest trial and greatest crisis.

Step out of the shadows. Step away from addiction and obsession. Step away from your hopeless romances and your foolish goals, which will have no promise in a future such as this. This is the challenge of your life, you see. Discount it at your own peril. Neglect it at your own peril. Argue with it at your own peril.

For technology will not save you. An alien race will not save you. They are part of your problem, you see. It is only human will, determination and cooperation that will fortify the human family in the great changes to come. It is your moral responsibility. It is your greater purpose for being here. It is what your life is really about.

Your service will not be grand. It will not garner great attention. It will be to help a person, or a group of people or a city or a town, wherever you are designed to give. The service must happen at all levels, in all ways from increasing numbers of people.

Do not wait until the skies grow dark and the waters rise and the lands dry out and the people are desperate. For then it will be too late to do much of anything, for yourself or for others.

God is giving you now the eyes to see, the ears to hear. You have this within you already, in a deeper Intelligence within you called Knowledge. It is beyond your intellect. It is more powerful than your intellect. It is greater than your ideas, your assumptions, your beliefs or your preferences.

You must face this greater reality. If you do not, your life will be wasted and forfeited, and your purpose will be unrecognized and unfulfilled.

Yet if you do face it, you will be frightened at first, but you will gain strength as you continue to recognize the great need that is emerging. It will help you re-evaluate your life and to give up little and dangerous and harmful things. It will be the perfect impetus and inspiration for you to bring your life and mind in order and to learn how to follow Knowledge, for that is the meaning of all true spirituality and all true religion.

God has given you a perfect guiding Intelligence. It is unafraid of the world. It is uncorrupted by the world. What other part of you can claim this, in all honesty? That which is weak within you must follow that which is strong. That which is weak within you must follow others who are strong in the way in which We speak.

Humanity has backed itself into a corner. There is no easy way out. There is no simple solution. There is no one technology that is going to change all this. Humanity does not know how to prepare. It only has little pieces of the preparation, and most of that has never been really tested before.

If you will give this your attention, it will help you to understand. If you will understand that you were sent here for this, it will bring your life into greater balance, and a greater strength can begin to emerge within you.

For the first time in human history, the Lord of all the universe has provided the Steps to Knowledge to the human family, an ancient teaching that has been given to other races in the universe over countless eons of time. It is this that must be studied, for this will engage you with the greater power within you, which is connected to God. Be you religious or not, no matter what your faith tradition, or if you have no faith tradition, it is all the same. The gift is the same. The need is the same. The truth is the same.

Argue with this theologically. Argue with it psychologically. Argue with it politically, economically. It does not matter. It is all a failure to respond. Do not defend your weakness in this way, but see that God is calling you through the Revelation to recognize the condition of the world and of your life, your future and your destiny here.

Do this for yourself. Do this for your children. Do this for everything you love and appreciate about the world. But beyond this, do this for those who sent you here, who are watching to see if you can respond.

The Messenger is in the world. He is an older man now. He will not be here forever. He holds part of the gift within himself, for he was sent from the Angelic Assembly, as [were] all of the former Messengers.

This is the time. This is the moment. This is the crisis. Only when you see you do not have an answer for these things will you turn to that which does have the answer and can lead you step by step to repositioning your life and your mind correctly so that you may have wisdom and clarity, instead of fear and admonition.

This is the Love that God is giving you. It is hard. It is challenging. It is uncomfortable. It is not merely to comfort and reassure you. It is to call you into service, into a greater service and recognition, into a greater cooperation between you and others—between groups, between religions, between nations, for the preservation and the advancement of humanity.

Many people will refuse. They will cling to their former beliefs and ideas and investments. They will blindly reject this as impossible, or think that this is the end times for humanity, and that all they must do is pray, when in fact they must prepare.

For this is the great transition. But great transitions, by their very nature, are difficult and hazardous. People can fail during such great turning points. And failure here would be more costly than anything you have ever experienced in this world. You cannot afford such things.

Heaven is watching to see who can respond, who will prepare, who will bring their life in order and take the Steps to Knowledge and build the Four Pillars of their life—the Pillar of Relationships, the Pillar of Work, the Pillar of Health, the Pillar of Spiritual Development—the Four Pillars upon which any true life must stand and can be stable in turbulent and uncertain times.

This is the Calling. This is true Love. If there were not true Love, the Creator of all life would look away and let humanity fall into chaos and dissolution, only to be overtaken by foreign powers, who are far more cruel and harsh than anything you can imagine.

Do not give up. Do not give in. Do not capitulate to your own fears or to the challenges around you. Do not be a victim. Be a contributor. Here you will gain strength and purpose and renewal. For only a greater situation now can restore and renew and prepare humanity to face the great challenges that are to come.

God's New Revelation for the world is the largest Revelation ever given, given now to a world community—a literate community, a world of global commerce, a world of growing global awareness, a world of global communication.

It is the greatest opportunity before things really begin to break down. It is the greatest time, you see. It is the time of your life. Respond to this and you will begin to make your great return to your Source, to your purpose and the greater destiny that has brought you here, under these very circumstances that We speak of.

The Messenger is in the world. Learn of him. Assist him if you can. Receive from him. He is the only one who can bring God's Revelation into the world. When he is done, the Seal of the Prophets will close behind him, and nothing more will be given for a very long time.

It is because of this that his Message is so great and so detailed, so repetitive, so broad, so inclusive, so directly important to every aspect of your life; given over a great period of time, given with its own commentary, so its truth is not left up to future commentators, who did not know the Messenger and who likely did not understand the Revelation. There can be no confusion now. The mistakes of the past cannot be repeated in how the great Revelations are used and employed.

Everything is important now. Every day is important. Every decision is important. Your decision, the decision of others, your behavior, the behavior of others—everything is important now. Your life is important now, but only within this greater context.

Failure must be avoided and resisted at all costs, for to face the Great Waves of change will cost everything. Instead of building larger armies and enriching a few individuals, all the resources of your societies and nations will have to be brought to bear.

Face the Power and the Presence, and Grace will attend you. You can overcome your weakness and your fear because there is a greater power within you. In God's New Revelation for the world, this power is made most evident and necessary.

CHAPTER 3

THE GLOBAL EMERGENCY

As revealed to
Marshall Vian Summers
on October 20, 2015
in Boulder, Colorado

Humanity is at the threshold of great global change, world change on a scale never seen before, caused now by humanity's misuse and overuse of the world, by human ignorance and human greed. It is a condition now that will affect the lives of every person.

Though few are yet aware of it, it is a global emergency. You have changed the chemistry of the atmosphere, of the waters and the soils. And now the world is changing—changing so rapidly, so dangerously, changing now in ways that will affect you more than you realize.

God's Message for the world must sound the alarm and provide the preparation for a new world reality. It is a time and a threshold that will call upon many to arise out of their self-preoccupied lives, out of their personal misery and confusion, to serve a world in peril.

This is one of the reasons why there is Intervention from the universe beyond you because those who value this world for themselves recognize what is taking place. They have tested the atmosphere of the world. They understand what humanity has done to pollute its air, its waters and its soil. For this has happened countless times in the universe. It is well understood there. So there is a race now to gain control of the world, to preserve it for the use of those from beyond. They are directly connected to this, you see.

It is a global emergency on a scale you have not yet realized. It has the power to destroy human civilization. It has the power to generate intervention from beyond. It has the power to create chaos here at a level never seen before.

You are going to have to follow a deeper power within yourself now, for increasingly there will be friction all around you and friction all around the world as human communities are stressed to a breaking point; as ancient animosities now begin to overflow and engulf nations and regions; as the competition for the remaining resources becomes fierce and dangerous, producing conflict and aggravation on a scale never seen before.

To some, it will look like the end of the world, a fulfillment of an ancient prophecy, as if it is all the work of God. But God is not the author of this global emergency. God is the witness. This is the product of humanity's ignorance and selfishness and shortsightedness and lack of understanding of the future and the consequences of its actions.

God must now warn the human family of the great peril it has created, of the great calamity that it has set in motion. For within this time, humanity can prepare and can mitigate the consequences of its actions.

If it fails to do this, then human civilization will be imperiled everywhere, in every nation. Economies will be ruined. Millions of people will be out of work. Millions of people will have to leave their homelands, which have become barren and uninhabitable.

That is why God's New Revelation for the world must sound this alarm, must give this warning. You have changed the climate of the world. It is [now] changing on its own. It will continue to change. It will produce drought and floods and deprivation. It will ruin the economies of nations that have to deal with the consequences and the events—the calamities that now will be ever more frequent and ever more destructive.

It is a time when humanity will have to unite to protect the world and to save itself. God is here giving you the warning, the blessing and the preparation to save yourselves, to save your nation, to save your families and your communities, to save human civilization.

You cannot afford to descend into chaos, for that would use up the remainder of the world's resources, leaving a degree of impoverishment you cannot imagine.

The Angelic Assembly that oversees this world has seen this coming. And it is approaching so quickly now, accelerating itself and being further accelerated by humanity's continuing to contaminate the air, the waters and the soil—setting in motion forces that you do not even fully understand; setting in motion forces of change and upheaval that will work against humanity, that will threaten humanity now.

It is the race to save human civilization. It is a race that must be run. It is the calling for human cooperation and unity to face a reality never seen here on the Earth before in the time of human civilization.

God knows what is coming. The Assembly knows what is coming if humanity does not prepare. For this has happened countless times in the universe where rare and beautiful worlds such as this are destroyed and ruined by the ignorance of their native population, exploited and plundered and contaminated to a degree where the natural environment begins to decline.

You cannot afford this. You must see this. You must face this. You must have the courage, the honesty and the humility to face this. Only a great peril now, only a great tribulation, only a great opportunity for human unity and cooperation, born now of necessity, will call for God to speak to the world again.

The hour is late. Humanity has delayed far too long. It is a crisis foreseen by those who are prescient and well informed. Do not think there are any other problems facing humanity that can compete with what We are saying here today. Do not think there is another great need or requirement that surpasses what We are saying here today. It is a great warning. It is upon you.

The coastal cities and ports of the world could be flooded in 30 years. The lands will dry out. The crops will fail. There will be human migration on a scale never seen, with great tribulation and conflict arising. It will be an overwhelming situation if humanity does not prepare.

It is the most important thing in the world. It will require all of humanity's resources, talents, skills and cooperation to contend with this and to secure humanity's future in a world that has now been changed and made more difficult and made more hazardous. It will be the greatest human endeavor in the history of this world.

But humanity must unite. It must end its ceaseless conflicts and its destructive competition to collaborate now, or nations will fall like dominoes. And their crisis will be so overwhelming, it will surpass the capacity of humanity to deal with it in the future if humanity cannot and will not prepare. We have spoken of this repeatedly, but the crisis is growing. Escalating, it is.

God loves humanity, or God would look the other way and allow the bitter fruits of your actions to confront you and overtake you. But God loves this world and seeks to make it a free and advancing nation in the universe, where freedom is rare and where worlds such as this are rare and so difficult to find.

Races from beyond the world have faced these situations. It is well known, and that is why exploitation of the Earth now and Intervention are being carried on with such determination, carried on without the use of force. For these few nations who are engaged in this do not want to further degrade the world through conflict and will rely upon human labor and cooperation to succeed in gaining control here. They do not want to destroy humanity, but to use humanity for their own purposes. And since conquest is not allowed in this part of the universe, other means must be sought: deception and persuasion—far greater weapons than you realize.

People are self-consumed. They are self-possessed. The rich are caught in a web of greed and confusion and disappointment. The poor are struggling to survive with ever-greater difficulty. The governments are committed to maintaining a reality that can only further degrade the world.

Do not think this will be easy. Do not think it will require only a few things to alter the course that humanity is currently on. Do not think there are easy and basic solutions. There are a thousand solutions that will be needed, and you only have a few. You will have to find the others, and it will take great human effort and collaboration to make this possible.

You are living in a global emergency. Do not think this will not affect you and your life profoundly and completely. It can ruin your economies. It can lead to mass starvation and death. It can lead to warfare, perpetual warfare, on a scale that has never been seen here before. It can create calamities so violent and continuous, as if nature were thrashing out against humanity, imperiled now by what it [humanity] has created—the world it has created, the change it has created, the destruction it has created—wrought upon other life and now upon itself.

This is a calling for every nation, every religion. God has provided the core preparation, which must occur if humanity will have the courage, the determination and the vision to see what must be done, to take the action that must be taken and to build the cooperation that must be built.

It is not enough to just focus on ending poverty, or bringing greater justice where it is needed in so many places. It is not enough to just use the world more wisely. It is not enough to cease pollution alone.

You are going to have to cool the planet—a task far beyond what has ever been achieved, but still achievable. But it will require a radical redistribution of resources, a redirection of human will and purpose, a great utilization of all of humanity's science and capabilities.

You are going to have to cool the planet. It will change everything that humanity is doing right now. You will have to replant the forests and restore the soils and cleanse the rivers. People will have to live very simply, for all the wealth of the world will be spent on this.

There is nowhere to hide for the wealthy. There is no real insulation for the privileged; for all that they have will be threatened by the things We speak of here today.

It is the great Love of God that is bringing you this warning. Do not think it is exaggerated in any way, for We are not even telling you everything. And We are not telling you everything because you do not yet have the capacity, the courage or the determination to hear it and face it.

Many will ignore what We are telling you. Many will not respond. And they will be washed away when the Great Waves strike—unaware, unprepared—for they did not see it coming, and they would not heed the warning, and they would not recognize the signs.

Change your life. Simplify your life. Use as little of the world's resources as you can. Collaborate. Forgive. Know what is happening in your world. See the great crisis coming over the horizon. Look with objective and honest eyes with as much courage as you can muster.

God has given you the great strength and determination to rise to this occasion—the greatest occasion in all of human history, an occasion that will determine the future of every person, and of your children and your future generations. God has given you the power and the determination at the level of Knowledge, the Knowledge that lives within you beyond the surface of your mind, beyond your intellect and all of its preoccupations and complaints.

It is at this level that people must be ignited, or they will not have the courage and the determination, the courage or the honesty or the compassion to face something of this magnitude. And that is why

God is giving you the key, the secret ingredient, the one thing that will make all the difference—all the difference in your life as an individual and all the difference in the life of humanity as a whole. For God has put a deeper Knowledge within you. And this is not corrupted or contaminated by the world and all of its illusions and tragedies, its misery and its degradation.

God has given you the strength that you will need, and it is provided in God's New Revelation for the world, perhaps the most important Revelation ever given—given now to save humanity from itself; given now to save human civilization; given now to redeem all those who can respond to it; given now with great urgency, great warning, but also with the great Blessing of the Creator. For God does not want to see you fail at the hour of greatest need.

Do not withdraw into your fearful little life. Do not step back into the shadows. Do not preoccupy yourself with little things or foolish romances that have nowhere to go in a changing world.

This is a calling to rise to the greatest occasion in history. It is a calling of a need so great and so profound. If you were to recognize it even partially, it would completely alter your priorities, your actions and your intentions.

The Great Waves of change will reveal human corruption, human delusion, human ignorance and stupidity. But they also have the power to generate a force so strong that humanity's greater strength, greater purpose and greater endowment from the Creator can be activated and brought into great service to the world.

But to see the solution, you must see the challenge. You must see the global emergency. And you must be part of it, for you are part of it.

You must find your place and your role. You must be prepared through the Revelation. You must gain the eyes to see and the ears to hear. If you can do this, your individual role will begin to emerge slowly as you bring your life into order and as you gain the vision to see what is occurring in your world and in your life.

Do not seek enlightenment. Do not seek to escape, for there is no escape. There is only contribution and collaboration, or there is failure and catastrophe.

Let this be your understanding.

CHAPTER 4

THE PLIGHT OF HUMANITY

As revealed to
Marshall Vian Summers
on July 26, 2009
in Beirut, Lebanon

The growing storms of the world, the growing plight of humanity, are being driven by the Great Waves of change now—change that is encompassing nations and peoples everywhere, a world where an ever-growing population will be drinking from a slowly shrinking well.

The world is overwhelmed. People are being forced together in ever greater numbers, different groups occupying the same environment— competing for power, armed, contentious with each other, with different agendas, different alliances, small nations being used by larger nations to provoke competition for land, for water, for food, not just for power and influence, but for the very basic things that everyone requires.

Into these growing storms now, humanity is moving—unprepared, unaware, not realizing the Great Waves of change that now are beginning to impact the human family. Many places now are facing the impact of these Great Waves more powerfully as ever greater numbers of people swell the teeming cities, where groups that are armed and contentious make tenuous truces with one another.

The greater problem facing all will require a level of cooperation and the ending of conflict, but not enough people see this and know this and are willing to sacrifice their position, to sacrifice their agenda. It is still perceived that armed conflict can win the day, that one group can overwhelm another and drive them away. But it is too late for that, you see, for there is nowhere to go now.

The world is full. The world cannot carry any more, but there are more and more. The wealthy carry on their little play and their fantasies and their indulgences while people blocks away are struggling to survive—a kind of suicidal activity, you see. It is in these environments, then, that the tragedy and the plight of humanity will play itself out in the early stages of the Great Waves of change.

The world is changing. The climate has now been disrupted. Humanity will lose much of its natural security. Food and water will become more precious and more difficult to obtain. The stresses will be felt, even in the wealthy nations that seem so insulated from the plight of humanity.

But who can see and who can know? Who has the eyes to see and the compassion to look without condemnation? Without cynicism? Who can simply look and see? Can wealth and poverty really coexist to this extent without leading to a kind of collapse?

Those who have time and the luxury to reconsider their lives and circumstances, and to change and alter the course of their lives, they must now look and see and stop pretending that technology or politics or some other avenue will maintain their insulation and their affluence in the ways that they have known. This is a time to be really honest. It is a time of reckoning. It is a time to prepare, for those who have the luxury to do so.

What you will see in the coming years and decade will be so shocking and so disheartening. Though humanity will make progress in many areas, its overall condition is deteriorating.

This is why God has sent a New Message into the world, you see, for human civilization is now at risk. Humanity is faltering. It is entering a time of great travail. It is entering a time where the fruits of its ignorance and competition and conflict will bear out. It is a time where people will have to choose whether they will unite and cooperate to save their communities and their nation or whether they will fight and struggle and maintain their ancient animosities, using politics and religion as a pretense, when in fact it is a struggle for resources.

Those who live in relative freedom and affluence will have to become the great contributors now, for the poor will become ever more endangered, and the tensions will rise as the struggle to live becomes more acute.

It is not a question of looking with love or with fear. It is a question of seeing, a question of responsibility.

The rich will continue their play and all of the justifications and excuses they will make. Yet they will fall as the pillars of their nations collapse, as the angry poor, the great swell of humanity, turn against them. They will retreat and abandon the faltering countries, but the plight is worldwide now. Go to the most pleasurable place on Earth, and you will see the plight of humanity growing.

What will money and wealth provide in the face of this? Certainly, it will give security and insulation for a time, but even the pillars of wealth will begin to fall, for their basis is false. This is occurring already, as humanity as a whole becomes poorer and more destitute.

This is why the Creator of all life has sent a New Message, because the ancient Messages have been too altered and have become the province of political forces and national interests and commercial investments. They have an interest in maintaining the plight of humanity. Despite the purity of their faith, it has become too immersed in the world, too corrupted by selfish interests and political aims.

So a New Message has been sent for humanity—a warning, a blessing and a preparation. If you cannot heed the warning, you will not understand the blessing, and you will not receive the preparation. If you cannot see, then you cannot know. If you cannot know, then your actions will be foolish and ill advised.

But who today can receive a New Message from God? So many people think that all the Messages have been given—there is nothing more for God to say to the world; God has lost interest in the world; for centuries God is doing something else; there is nothing left to say.

But how can this be when humanity has reached a new threshold, a great turning point where all of human civilization is at risk, where the eyes of your competitors in the universe now look at the world, seeing the opportunity to intervene, to gain influence, to undermine the weakness of humanity?

The great traditions of the world have nothing to say about this. They can only admit that God would have to give some kind of new instruction. And in this, they are correct. God is giving a new instruction through the Angelic Presence who oversees the world.

For humanity is entering a new phase, a dangerous phase, a cataclysmic phase, but also a phase of great promise. For it is under these deteriorating situations and conditions that there is a chance that real human unity and cooperation will become established, not merely out of principle, but out of sheer necessity. If humanity cannot unite in its prosperity, then it must unite in the loss of its prosperity.

People have made technology their god. They think technology will solve all of these problems and all of the problems that technology will create. But technology is based on resources, and the resources are diminishing in the world. Humanity has depleted the world now to a point where it cannot rely upon technology to save it, for ever-growing numbers of people in the world will not be able to benefit from this.

The world's soils have been depleted and destroyed by technology and by ignorance. The world's fisheries are depleted. And now the world's climate is changing, becoming unpredictable and destructive.

What will humanity do in the face of this? Its self-assurances certainly will be seen as inadequate. Those who give warning will be dismissed as being extreme. People want to hear good news. They want to be reassured because they are too weak and unstable to face reality.

The governments are not preparing their people for the Great Waves of change. Religious leaders are not preparing people for the Great

Waves of change. So the people are weak and unprepared and only seek assurances.

Around the world, people are praying to God for deliverance, for security, for improving conditions and improving relationships between nations. And God has responded in a New Message for humanity, but who can accept that this is true? Surely the Message will be unlike people's expectations because the Creator of all life is not bound by these things.

What will be given to humanity is what humanity needs, not what humanity wants or expects. Everyone wants more wealth, more possessions, more security, but the world cannot deliver. People want to be richer. The rich want to be richer. The poor want to have stability and security, which they need. But for this to be possible now, there must be a great equitable sharing of the world.

Humanity will have to control its population and its consumption of resources. Who has the wisdom, the power and the restraint to do this?

If you are clear, if you are honest, you can see what is required. So what will it take for this awareness to become shared and certain, overriding people's preferences, their religious beliefs, the supremacy of their national interests? How much suffering and destruction must take place before there is an honest reckoning of what is really required?

Do not condemn other peoples or nations if you yourself are not willing to accommodate the Great Waves of change and to adapt to them and to prepare for them. Who are you to make such criticism? So easy it is to blame others and to not see your own limitations.

How great must the Great Waves of change become before they overwhelm people's military objectives, their political agendas and their racial and cultural isolation? How great must the Waves become? Do nations have to collapse? Must there be immense war and genocide? What will it take until there is a different kind of awareness, an honest reckoning of the situation?

Who in the world today knows that humanity is being watched from others in the universe, your neighbors who seek to take advantage of a weak and divided humanity? If nations understood this, war would cease. They would prepare humanity to safeguard the world.

What humanity sees and what humanity must see are not yet even close. That is why there is a New Message from God because time is of the essence. You do not have decades or a century to prepare, for the Great Waves are moving, and Intervention into the world has already begun.

The poor are so overworked and so overwhelmed, they cannot see. Their governments are too obsessed with their agendas. No one is looking ahead. No one is considering the future. That is why there is a New Message from God.

God's great Revelations from the past have given great clarification about the ethics and the behavior that individuals must assume to live well and to live in harmony with others. These great Messages that are so essential and have played a part in the building of human civilization and the advancement of humanity are not sufficient to meet the great needs that are now emerging. That is why God has sent a New Revelation and a Messenger into the world to provide this Revelation.

If you are honest, you will see you do not have an answer. You do not have an answer to the Great Waves of change. You do not have an answer to Intervention into the world by those races who seek to influence human thinking and behavior. You do not have an answer for the shrinking well. You can only make assumptions, and these assumptions, for the most part, have no validity. For the world has changed, but people have not changed with it.

Your crisis will be when you realize the enormity of the Great Waves of change and your inability to provide an answer. But God has provided an answer through you and through all others, an answer that will be activated by God's New Revelation. For there is a deeper Intelligence within you that must be activated, and nothing else can really activate it except the Power of the Creator and all the forces that are here to serve humanity's well-being and advancement.

People's notions about religion and the final judgment are so false, so ridiculous—the projections of an ignorant people. God wills that humanity survive the Great Waves of change and advance and unite and maintain and build human freedom and creativity in the process.

But this is such a goal, it seems almost unattainable given everything that you are facing. That is because you are thinking with your intellect, which is a product of the past, and not with the deeper Intelligence that God has placed within you that can lead you through the difficult times ahead.

It is as if the human family needs an upgrade, a shift in reality, a different set of assumptions, a different mandate, a different understanding. Without this, humanity will continue its ignorant pursuits, its destructive use of the world, competition between nations, sowing the seeds of future war and conflict.

For nations to survive and to be stable, they must cooperate. Even where they are ancient enemies, the resources that are essential—the energy, food and water—must be shared and provided. Human populations must be brought under some humane control. And there will have to be control of the use of resources and the consumption of resources.

Every advanced nation in the universe has had to do this to survive. It is now time for humanity to grow up, to outgrow its adolescent behavior, its irresponsible behavior, its unaccountable behavior, and start preparing for the future so that you will have a future.

If you exhaust the resources of the world, you will not be able to go out in the universe to find them, for they are owned by others. If you should become so weak and vulnerable, then the power of persuasion that will be cast over the world will be so strong, you cannot deny it. You cannot refuse it. For your position will be too weak and unstable.

These ideas seem so extreme. They seem so different. It is because humanity is still thinking like a primitive people. It is still thinking that the world is endless, that the resources are endless and that it is alone in a dark universe.

But the world is limited, and you are reaching those limits, and the universe is full of life—a competitive environment on a scale you cannot even imagine. You see the difference here between these words and this understanding and the way you think and how you see the world, and how you see humanity's future, and how you see the prospect of life in the universe?

What can create this new awareness but a New Message from the Creator of all life? You know not what you are preparing for. You know not what is coming over the horizon. Even your most highly educated individuals cannot see and do not know.

There must be a New Revelation for humanity. You are living in a time of Revelation. God knows this. God knows what humanity needs, what humanity must see and do. But what God knows and what people think are so very different.

In the face, then, of the plight of humanity and the growing storms of the world, a New Message is being sent here, a Message that calls upon the strength of the individual and the collective strength of people. It is not just a Message of hope. It is a Message of necessity. It is not just a Message of a wonderful afterlife. It is a Message to prepare humanity to survive the Great Waves of change and to protect its freedom and sovereignty in this world as it emerges into a Greater Community of intelligent life in the universe. It is not a Message about miracles and fantastic creation stories and judgment days and the prospect of Heaven and Hell. You have more important things to concern yourself with now. And this is what God's New Message emphasizes.

God does not favor one religion over another, but God hears the yearning and the sincere requests for help. Whether they come from the religiously oriented or from the secular population, God knows the plight of humanity. All races in the universe reach a point such as this if they are technologically evolving. And you have reached this point where you either destroy yourself or you begin to build a new platform for human existence.

Here you choose either domination or freedom. Most nations in the universe have chosen domination. That is why freedom is rare. But freedom is the choice you must make. It is what will assure humanity the greatest power and the greatest security in the universe.

But it will be a long, long road to reach this new stability and a tremendous re-assessment, re-evaluation, a tremendous responsibility not just for leaders of nations, but for citizens everywhere.

People will need each other to survive and to produce this greater foundation. It is this God's New Message emphasizes for the world.

You must listen to a different voice within yourself—not the voice of your cultural values, the voice of your prejudices, the voice of your intellectual pride, the voice of your sense of security, your assumptions of power. What are these but nothing?

There is a deeper voice you must learn to listen to, or you will not hear God's New Message. You will not hear the suffering of the world, and you will not see the signs of the world that are telling you what is coming over the horizon. God's New Message will teach you to find this deeper voice, for this will be essential and central to humanity's redemption and to securing humanity's future as a free race in the universe.

CHAPTER 5

THE RACE TO SAVE HUMAN CIVILIZATION

As revealed to
Marshall Vian Summers
on July 22, 2009
in Aleppo, Syria

While everything appears to be normal in these days, Great Waves of change are coming to the world, change on a level never seen before, change that will affect every person in the world. Greater than the world wars, it will be. Greater than the great pandemics of the past will it be, Great Waves of change, as humanity has plundered the world and has destroyed your natural inheritance to such a great degree that the world will change now, becoming a more difficult place for the human family.

It has taken a very long time to create the conditions that will bring about the Great Waves of change. And everyone has participated in this to some degree, so there is no one person or organization or nation alone who is fully to blame. The wealthy nations have taken more, but everyone has taken from the world—even the poorest people, who have taken so little and who have so little. Everyone is responsible.

It is a situation now that you must consider for the future and prepare for at this time. For there will be great human migrations as the arid regions of the world lose their ability to produce food, as water resources become scarce and as conflict arises between nations and groups within nations over who will have access to the remaining resources. However masked these conflicts may be under the guise of religion and politics, it will be a struggle for resources primarily.

The world sounds the same—the vibrations and noise of a big city. It is but the signs of great change to come that people are not seeing because they are not responding to Knowledge, the deeper Intelligence that the Creator of all life has placed within each person to guide them, to protect them and to lead them to their greater accomplishments in life.

Millions of people will have to flee the arid regions of the world. Coastal regions will be flooded and impacted by tremendously powerful storms and violent weather. People will have to move due to economic reasons—failure of local economies and in some cases national economies.

Where will they all go, these people, who did not see and did not recognize? Who will accept them into their nation? Who will accept the floods of thousands and millions of people who must now leave their homelands or who must relocate within their own nation?

The social disruption will be immense. The political tension will be immense. The call for compassion and the ending of grievances will be immense. This will be a humanitarian tragedy and a humanitarian need on a scale never seen before.

For the world cannot afford to descend into chaos, or humanity will not have a future. Really, what is at stake here is rescuing human civilization. Human civilization that seems so dominant, so powerful, so well established today, tomorrow and the days to come will seem ever more fragile and vulnerable.

It is really now a race to save human civilization from collapse and ruin. This is something that any person can see once they are alerted to the Great Waves of change, once they begin to listen to the sounds of the world and see the signs that the world is producing. People today feel already that things are not normal, things are not right. There is great anxiety concerning people's view of the future.

Already the Great Waves are beginning to impact the peoples of the world, diminishing nations' economies, forcing people into ever greater situations of strain and competition. Even today there is a great struggle for who will have access to the food, the water and the energy resources in many, many parts of the world.

Yet who is watching the signs, the signs that Great Waves of change are now coming? Who is paying attention? And for those very few who are, who has the courage and the strength to recognize that this is a calling—a calling for service and contribution; a calling for them to reconsider their lives, their circumstances, their activities and their obligations?

Human migration will be one of the great problems that the Great Waves of change will produce. In the teeming cities in the poorer nations, where will these people go, and how will they be sustained? Will they be left to die, to emerge into war and famine? This is something that a few people in the world today are beginning to consider because the signs are so very evident.

It is not the end for humanity, but it is a transition to a different kind of world—a new world, a world of declined resources, a world of diminished assets, a world that will require tremendous cooperation between nations if human civilization is to survive.

The peoples who will have to flee the stricken areas, they will have to be absorbed by nations around the world. They cannot simply move next door because the nation next door is likely to be facing the same crisis. It will be a great diaspora, a dispersion of peoples out of their homeland away from their traditional way of life into a very different set of circumstances. This will produce greater strain and difficulty.

Primary here, amongst this, is literally how will you feed the peoples of the world when the world loses 30 percent of its agriculture, which is what you are really facing, you see? Violent weather, the change in the climate and the impact upon the world's geologic and biologic systems will create so much imbalance that even if you could find a home for all the displaced peoples, how would you feed them? And the residents of the receiving nations, how will they respond to all this?

These are questions that have yet to be answered, questions that you should now consider—you who stand at the threshold of great change, you who perhaps have the luxury to consider these things and to plan your life and to rearrange your priorities.

The cities will become so filled with people that it will be very difficult to provide food and water for them, even in the well-established countries, even in countries where there is greater affluence. How will you feed a million new people added to a city of millions already? The teeming city, you can hear the sounds. How much can a city hold? What are the limits of its provision? What is the tolerance of its people?

The situation will become so severe that even families in the wealthy nations will have to consider taking a family from a poor nation into their home. How many people will be willing to do this? How bad does it have to get before people's preferences and prejudices and personal requirements are superseded by a critical need?

There will not be enough surplus food to simply ship it out to stricken nations. There will not be enough. If humanity loses a percentage of its food production, it does not matter how much money is spent.

The world is being exhausted. Are you going to exhaust it even more and more and more? This is the great uncertainty in the situation—how will humanity respond? What is human response-ability? Even the leaders of nations are blind. Even the leaders of religious institutions are blind. They only see the world as they are accustomed to see the world. They only see the world in terms of what they can expect and believe to be true from the past. But these things will no longer hold true.

There will be great human migration all over the world. Some of it will be normal, but much of it will have to be organized and agreed to between nations. If nations close their doors to the displaced peoples, it will be a tragedy never seen before. This tragedy will despoil the world in war and conflict.

All of this is inevitable, you see, given humanity's attitudes and use of the world and humanity's relations between nations. Of course, you would reach a point of saturation. Of course, you would affect the world in such a way that the world would respond not to your benefit. Of course, you would hit a crisis point.

There are visionary individuals who have seen this coming. But humanity is deaf and blind and dumb and proceeds willfully in its pursuits of wealth and power—easily corrupted, easily misled, desperate amongst its poorer peoples, unable to control its population, unable to control its use of resources, unable to restrain its conflicts and its historical prejudices. Like a willful child, it is going headlong into the future—heedless, not thinking ahead, not looking ahead, only meeting the needs of the day.

At this moment, you can stand in the middle of a city of two million people and in 20 years, it will be desolate. What will happen? How will the world respond?

If you can see without prejudice and fear, it will become apparent to you. You do not have to be a genius to see this. You only have to be wise and objective. But how people will respond is a question that you cannot foretell. For people can choose how they will respond. There is choice at this level.

You cannot stop the Great Waves of change. You can mitigate them and their impacts, and you can prepare for them, but you cannot stop them now.

If people cannot change, based upon their conscience and their vision of the world, then they will have to change in the face of demanding situations and crises. It is a poor way of learning, of course. It is a fool's education, of course. But the education must happen because humanity must adapt to a world in change, to a declining world.

The poorer peoples of the world, what can they do now to prepare? They have no social power, no social mobility. They cannot simply pack up and move to a wealthy nation. They are stuck. They are held in place. So the responsibility lies with the wealthy peoples and the wealthy nations to lead the way. But even in the wealthy nations, there are few who can see. And people everywhere, rich or poor, are so often unwilling to reconsider their lives and to change their attitudes and approaches. It is a problem in human development.

The world will become warmer. Lands will open up, but you will not be able to grow much food on them. And violent weather will be a problem everywhere—depleting nations' resources, creating catastrophes one after another.

Humanity will have to move to a different kind of equilibrium with life in the future, a different kind of stability in the world. The great question facing you is what will happen between now and then? If people are blind and do not see the Great Waves of change coming over the horizon; if people are unwilling to reconsider their lives, their obligations and their circumstances; if people are unwilling to overlook their cultural and national prejudices and grievances, then humanity is heading towards a great calamity, or series of calamities to be more precise.

The man or woman of Knowledge sees this, of course. They are not in denial. They are not simply trying to project a preferred outcome. They are seeing what is transpiring, and they are altering their conclusions regularly as the situation changes, as the Great Waves approach. For you may be certain that the Great Waves are coming, but you do not know how they will impact the world or when they will strike. And the great uncertainty is how humanity will respond.

So the man or woman of Knowledge is watching—watching without coming to fixed conclusions, watching without condemning the world, watching without losing hope, watching without becoming jaded or cynical, watching without blaming leaders or individuals or nations, watching the changing landscape of the world, looking for the signs that the world is giving to indicate how and where and when the Great Waves will strike.

The man or woman of Knowledge has moved to higher ground, both circumstantially in their outer life and within themselves, basing their life upon Knowledge, the deeper Intelligence—an Intelligence that is not afraid of the world, that is not afraid of change, that can face anything because it is Intelligence given by God. It is wise. It is compassionate. It is objective.

Here the man or woman of Knowledge is not insisting on solutions, but instead watching and encouraging positive behavior, positive awareness, positive actions, but not reliant on hope alone, for hope is too weak, too easily shattered, too easily diminished and deflated.

Their power is the power of Knowledge—a power that does not diminish in the face of difficulty or uncertainty, a power that is not undermined by tragedy or crisis. They will see clearly and respond appropriately to the changing situations that they see immediately around them and in the world at large, for they are not afraid to look and to see because Knowledge is their power.

For everyone else, there will be denial in general. Then the few people who see the gravity of the situation will base all of their hope upon certain solutions being generated and applied. This will be the source of their hope, but it is a weak foundation. For their whole basis of certainty is based upon certain events taking place and certain changes being made. But these events may not take place. This change may not occur. Then where will they be, but in a state of despair? For their foundation is based upon circumstances, not upon the power of Knowledge.

They will believe in certain leaders who they think will save the day. But there is no leader in the world that can stop the Great Waves of change. They will believe in the goodness of humanity, but humanity will act very poorly, especially at the outset of the Great Waves. They will believe in an ideology or an economic system or technology or the advancements in science, but as these prove to be inadequate and insufficient, their hope will collapse.

Do you see how weak this is, how it is based upon either ideas or abstractions or upon certain situations occurring, which in reality may be very unlikely to occur? Your optimism cannot be based upon a preferred outcome.

The world is changing. You must change with it. You must move with it. You must watch it. Like a ship captain at sea, you must watch the weather and the waves. You must look at the barometer. You must adjust your sails accordingly. You cannot sit back idly and believe that everything will work out fine, for that is only a hope that masks fear and uncertainty. And fear and uncertainty will sink the ship.

That is why you must have a foundation in Knowledge. God has given you this to be your pilot, to be your guide, to be your compass. Without this, you only have dreams, hopes, wishes and fantasies to base your positive outlook on, and none of them will survive the Great Waves of change. You will be disappointed. You will be frustrated. You will be anguished. You will be angry. You will be disappointed, you see, because you had no foundation.

Technology will be important, but it will not save humanity. A political system may be preferred over another, but it will not save humanity. Nor will it be shared everywhere sufficiently to produce the cooperation and the assistance that will be required.

You must look ahead, with clear eyes, being willing to see whatever is coming over the horizon—without condemning it, without denying it, without drawing immediate conclusions. Like the captain of the ship at sea, you are watching and responding to changing circumstances.

You must have this inner security and strength of Knowledge to do this, or you will not be able to do it. You will go into denial. You will try to hide. You will try to live under a rock. You will put all your faith in some notion or ideology. You will dismiss the Great Waves as just a negative approach to life. You will be blind and foolish under the guise of being clever and intelligent.

Humanity's stupidity is most tragic when it is hidden behind a veneer of rationality and intelligence. You will see this all around you, of course. You will see the denial. You will see the projection of blame. You will see the wishful thinking. You will see the blind faith in science and technology, in good governance, or a particular leader.

People believe these things because they have no foundation. They have no real inner strength. They can endure hardship in the world, but they do not have the clarity of mind to see what is coming, what is heading their way, what will change their life. So they miss life's great opportunities. They miss life's signs. They miss life's warnings because they cannot look and see with clarity. It is a fundamental problem for each person.

People complain every day. Some people complain constantly. But complaining is not seeing. Complaining is not following the changing circumstances of your life. Complaining is like being a little baby who just cries and cries, or a little child that whines when it cannot get what it wants.

Therefore, you must stop complaining and start looking and develop the strength to look and watch, to clear your mind of judgment and condemnation. Take the Steps to Knowledge to build your connection to the deeper Intelligence that God has placed within you, for it is only this Intelligence that will save you, you see.

Human reason without Knowledge is just conventional thinking, blind and foolish, and unable to adapt to changing circumstances. If the world did not change, you could live on a certain set of assumptions. But you are facing the greatest change that humanity has ever faced, so these assumptions now will become real hazards for you and for everyone around you.

This warning is a gift of Love from the Creator of all life. It is part of a New Message for humanity to prepare humanity for the Great Waves of change, to prepare humanity for its encounter with intelligent life in the universe, to bring Knowledge and Wisdom into the world that has been developed elsewhere in the universe and to clarify humanity's relationship with the Divine and the real nature of human responsibility.

The future and the outcome are in the hands of every person because whatever happens will be the result of individuals making decisions. The question arises: What will inform those decisions? Will it be the power of Knowledge or will it be everything else that masquerades as power?

Do not think you have no power in this matter, for your future will be based on the decisions you make today and the actions you take today. It will be dependent upon the people you associate with and their influence upon you.

Therefore, God's New Message gives you great responsibilities, and it tells you that you cannot escape these responsibilities. Rich or poor, no matter what your circumstances, the power and the presence of Knowledge lives within you, waiting to be discovered. You need this now more than anything—more than wealth, more than security, more than comfort, more than pleasure, more than marriage, more than family, more than anything.

Without Knowledge, you will be blind. You will follow the panic and the obsessions of people around you. You will step into the future not knowing what you are facing. The Great Waves will overtake you. You will have not seen them coming.

This is the great calling for human awareness and responsibility now. You have time, but not much [time]. You have time to reconsider your life, but not much time. You have time to build a foundation in Knowledge, but not much time. You have time to gather your strength and your resources. You have time to begin to look from the watchtower at what is coming towards you, what is coming over the horizon—both in your local region and in the world at large.

Here instead of having intellectual discussions and theoretical conversations, you must prepare your life and prepare your primary relationships. Your grand ideology will mean nothing in the face of the Great Waves of change. A scholar can drown as well as a fool.

This is a powerful message to wake you, to snap you out of your preferential and conditioned thinking, your attitudes and assumptions, your beliefs and all that you avoid that you must now see.

God wills for humanity to survive and to advance in the face of the Great Waves of change, but what God wills and what people will do are not the same, you see. That is why God must send now a New Message into the world to prepare humanity for a future that will be unlike the past and to prepare you to not only survive the Great Waves of change, but to be a contributor within them, for that is why you have come into the world.

At a deeper level, you know this. It is clear. It has always been clear. At a deeper level, you knew you would enter the world at a time of great change and upheaval. There is no uncertainty here. There is no controversy here.

It is your purpose and mission now to become a contributor in the face of the Great Waves of change. But this awareness and this certainty occur at a deeper level in your mind, beneath the surface of your mind where you live and think and live out your days.

Therefore, We are calling for your responsibility, your accountability and your honesty—to be really truthful with yourself, to honor what you most deeply know, to discover it and what it means and how it will direct your life from this day forward. For this, you have Our blessings. For this, you have all the Power of Creation.

CHAPTER 6

STANDING AT THE PRECIPICE

As revealed to
Marshall Vian Summers
on April 10, 2014
in Boulder, Colorado

Without a New Message from God, the world's decline becomes predictable, devastating and tragic. Without a New Revelation from God to prepare humanity for the Great Waves of change that are coming, and for humanity's encounter with other races in the universe, which it is now facing, the decline of humanity becomes predictable. If enough people cannot receive God's New Revelation, this decline will continue. It is entirely preventable, but the hour is late.

Yet God's Revelation is in the world, given to prepare humanity for these two great thresholds; given to incite a deeper awareness, a deeper conscience, a deeper purpose in enough people to turn the tide, to give humanity the opportunity to prepare for a new world experience.

God knows this, of course, but people are unprepared. Beyond being unprepared, they are also ignorant and unwilling to learn—thinking that they know what reality is, relying upon their experience from the past, not realizing they stand at the threshold of great change.

The prophecy of the Great Waves of change has been given as part of the New Revelation. The preparation for this, for the individual, has been given as part of the Revelation. A clear picture must now be made of this future world should this preparation not be heeded sufficiently, should God's New Revelation be ignored or denied. You must understand here what you will be looking at and facing in the times to come and what your children will have to face as a consequence, and the generations beyond them.

God only speaks to humanity at times of great opportunity, times of great change, times where the history of the world can be altered—the seeds being planted in enough people to set in motion greater forces, greater powers, to be used for either good or ill. But now humanity stands at a threshold unlike any it has ever had to face—a changing environment, a changing climate, a world of diminishing resources, a world of growing economic and political instability.

If humanity were a wise race, they would have been preparing for decades for this. It would have been recognized. It would have been foreseen sufficiently, and sacrifices would have been made and preparations long established.

But humanity is not yet a wise race. It does not understand the world it lives in and the limits of this world. It does not understand it lives within a Greater Community of life in the universe, where freedom is rare and where worlds such as this are highly valued by others. It is a race preoccupied with its past and with its current difficulties and obsessions.

Here those who are prescient, who can see and understand, who can recognize the forces that are moving the world, will feel alone and isolated for the most part and are unable to understand what must be done in these times, in the great times of preparation that you have remaining.

God understands this, of course, and that is why the Revelation is in the world. It will give you everything you need if you can respond, if you can prepare, if you can alter your understanding and your priorities sufficiently to undertake this preparation with success. But you must understand the alternative should you neglect this, should you avoid this. It is not an easy picture, but it must be understood.

In the coming decades, the climate will change more dramatically than is currently forecast. Nations will run out of resources. Food production will be curtailed because of great environmental impacts. Regional wars and revolutions will erupt but without resolution, leaving nations incapacitated to deal with even their current circumstances, yet alone the demands of the future. Religions will become more fractured and divided as people feel threatened and only want to associate with their group—their ethnic group, their social group, their religious group, in opposition to others, who also become polarized in the face of great change and uncertainty.

This begins a long period of decline and disintegration as nations now become more isolated, seeking alliances perhaps, but more regionally isolated, and unwilling or unable to assist one another through the great challenges to come. A growing humanity will face the loss in many places of food, water and energy necessary to sustain civilization as they have known it.

This is not a set of problems and converging situations that technology alone can resolve, for technology will be overwhelmed. These are the great converging waves of change, change happening on every level conceivable, all at once. This is the vulnerability that humanity has created over decades of neglect and irresponsibility.

Yet the Revelation is in the world. God has spoken again, for the first time in over a thousand years. The warning has been established. The blessing has been given to the real power that humanity has to navigate the difficult times ahead and what this could mean to build human unity and cooperation at a level never seen before in this world—built now out of sheer necessity, built now out of compassion and responsibility, built now in such a way that humanity has a chance, a great chance, but not a chance that will last forever.

For the outcome will be decided in the decades to come as to the kind of world humanity will face, and whether it will be able to withstand persuasion and intervention from the universe around it, which so often happens in times such as these when the native peoples become weak and conflicted.

Do not think you are here by accident, for you were sent into the world to face these situations, to add your necessary but small part. This is true for everyone in the world. And though half of humanity is so oppressed by poverty and religious and political oppression, they can seem to do very little, the calling is still there for all those who are able and free enough to respond.

If the situation were not so very dire, then God would not need to speak again. Humanity would have time and resources to understand the situation and to prepare accordingly. But you passed that threshold some time ago—unknowingly, unwittingly—and now it will be a race to the finish, the race to save human civilization.

If your environment becomes uninhabitable, all would be lost. This is a consequence of humanity's use of the world, its attempt to dominate nature and turn it to its will and ends. It is not a curse from God. It is a product of lack of vision, responsibility and cooperation here on Earth.

Therefore, God does not speak with condemnation, but with power and promise. For the hour is late, and humanity cannot be negligent. It cannot be foolish. It cannot be self-destructive in the face of such greater forces of change.

If you had the courage and the humility to face what is coming squarely, you would see that God must speak again. For the world's religions were not established to deal with these great thresholds. And they are so divided between themselves, and even within themselves, that they can never lead humanity forward. Their prescriptions were for ancient times, a world that really no longer exists. And though their wisdom is great and their ethics are important, God must speak again, or humanity will surely fail.

The Revelation will restore that which is wise within the individual, enough individuals who will then be able to exert their influence in the world and to prepare and to survive the Great Waves of change and to build a greater future beyond the thresholds that are to come.

It is great challenge that will unite humanity now, nothing less than this. It is great consequences, great times, that will lift people out of self-obsession and misery to higher levels of service in the world.

For each of you were sent into the world to live at these times, and the contribution that you have been given to give is within you now, but it exists beyond the realm of the intellect. It must be called forth from a Greater Power—the greater power within you and the Greater Power beyond you.

This is the time of Revelation. This is the great time of decision. This is a great time where humanity will have to choose the kind of future it wants, fully understanding the great risks that it now faces.

You cannot be idle in these times. You cannot be ambivalent, or reality will overwhelm you and bring great misfortune to your life.

The Messenger is in the world, but he remains unrecognized and unknown. He is doing everything he can to bring the Message forth, to speak to people, but they must have the eyes to see and the ears to hear, or they will be deaf and blind, unable to respond.

God now brings not merely an improvement to the human family, not merely a new message of hope and inspiration, but the very thing that will save the human family itself—from collapse within this world and from subjugation from forces from beyond. It is only dire circumstances that would bring such a Revelation into the world. And you are facing such circumstances at this moment.

Do not wait for the hard rain to fall or for the great drought or for the great storm to convince you that you are living at such a time, for those with the eyes to see can see over the horizon the great storms building there. They can hear the voice of Knowledge within themselves, the deeper Mind that God has put within them to guide them, to protect them and to lead them to a greater life of service and fulfillment in a world undergoing a great change.

To see the answer, you must recognize the need. It is shocking. It will be difficult to face at first. You will feel helpless and hopeless. But God's New Revelation is in the world, and God has sent you with the power to respond, waiting to be discovered within you.

You must then face the shock of the future, for you stand at the precipice of determining the kind of future it will really be. Without great cooperation between the nations now, humanity will fall into a cycle of endless conflict over who has access to the remaining resources. These conflicts will be desperate and far more destructive than anything you have seen thus far.

There must be great compassion, great acceptance, great tolerance for other peoples. For you will not merely help yourself in this situation. You will be called to assist others whose needs are profound and overwhelming. It is a time of great cooperation. It is a time of great service.

People are still trying to be happy and to have what they want, beyond meeting their basic needs in life. But there is a greater calling for them, and for you. The world is giving that calling now. Do not think of your future in terms of what would make you happy or be a pleasant vocation, but what the world needs that you could provide, where your talents, whatever they may be, may be of real service to people.

This will change your life. This will change your relationship with yourself—how you feel about yourself and others. It will change everything in the way that you see your life—its value and its meaning. For this is how God will restore you, through preparation and then great service to others—restoring your worldly mind through service to the deeper Mind within you, which is called Knowledge.

Those who have the eyes to see will see, and they will hear Our words and take them to heart deeply. Others will forget or dismiss them, thinking this is too radical, too challenging, too impossible, thinking life cannot really be like that. Pray for them, for they are weak and cannot yet respond.

It is those who can respond who will make all the difference, but they must respond fully. This is not a casual engagement. This is not a few simple things to do. This is something that will alter the course of your life, but so much better that you alter the course of your life rather than your circumstances overwhelm you and change your life beyond your control.

This is the Wisdom that comes from the great Love of the Creator, for God loves humanity and does not want to see the human family disintegrate and fail for reasons that it cannot yet see. This is the toughness and the durability of God's Love now being given to a whole world to rescue it from failure and collapse, and to prepare it for engaging in a universe full of intelligent life, of which humanity knows nothing at all.

Only a New Message from God could provide these things, for only God knows the nature of your heart and soul. Only God knows what life is like in the universe everywhere. Only God could prepare you—emotionally, mentally and practically—for the road ahead.

It is only by coming to the Revelation that you will come to see these things We speak of here today. You must make that approach. God wills to rescue you and your life, but you must make the approach.

The blessing is upon the world now, for God has spoken again. A great preparation has been given to the world, a great inspiration, and the foundation for true cooperation between peoples and nations—born of necessity, born of reality, born of the truth of why you are really in the world and what you are here to serve beyond your own personal interests and needs.

CHAPTER 7

FACING PLANETARY INSTABILITY

As revealed to
Marshall Vian Summers
on March 14, 2011
in Boulder, Colorado

Great change is coming to the world, and people around the world are feeling this and sensing this and seeing the evidence of this. But the great change exceeds people's concerns and expectations.

For humanity has disrupted the world so sufficiently that now you are facing a different kind of world—a new world, a world of different dimensions, a world that will be quite new to your experience in so many ways, a world with a new climate, a world of diminishing resources, a world of growing economic and political upheaval and conflict, a world of greater stress and uncertainty, a world of erupting situations and natural catastrophes, a world where your food production will decline with the changing climate.

It is a world that people are not prepared for, for people still think the future will be like the past. They assume the world will always be as they have expected it to be. They have invested themselves and their lives in the world being a certain way, but it is now changed. It is a different world, a new world.

God has sent you into the world to be in the world at this time, facing these circumstances. But what God has placed within you to prepare you and to equip you and to strengthen you for the difficult times ahead is something that resides beyond the realm and the reach of the intellect, in a deeper Intelligence called Knowledge.

At the surface of your mind, you are swept by the winds of the world. You are chaotic. Your life does not seem to have a true direction. You are influenced by so many things from the outside. Your life can feel chaotic, confused, disorganized, disintegrated, disregulated— however you may choose to describe it.

But at a deeper level beneath the surface of the mind, there is a greater Intelligence within you. This Intelligence is here to guide you, to protect you and to prepare you to live a greater life in service to living in a new world.

People are not aware of the greater Intelligence within them. Perhaps they have fleeting moments of intuition, fleeting moments of insight. Perhaps they foresee certain things in the moment, but they do not abide with these visions. Instead, they speculate about them and give them their own meaning and preference.

People are having little experiences of Knowledge, so many people, but they do not know and are unaware of the greater endowment that God has given them. They are still influenced by the consensus opinion or the views of certain individuals in positions of leadership. They want to believe and trust that everything will be fine. They want to live in the moment, and for the poorer people, they have to live in the moment.

Humanity collectively seems remarkably unprepared for the future, remarkably unresponsive to what is coming over the horizon, remarkably ignorant and foolish regarding their current pursuits and distractions.

You cannot be fooling around in the face of the Great Waves of change. Your life must be repositioned. Your awareness must be sharpened. You must have a greater objectivity and clarity that you bring to witnessing the events of the world. You cannot simply be terrified by them, or upset by them, or feel helpless and confused in the face of them. They are all signs, preparing you, telling you what you need to know and to reconsider about your life.

You have to prepare for an unstable world. It is a new preparation for most people. It requires a great and deep evaluation of where you are and what you are doing, the position of your life and what change you must bring to your outer circumstances.

But most profoundly and central to your needs is to build a connection to Knowledge, to take the Steps to Knowledge, for it is only Knowledge that can truly prepare you to navigate the difficult and unpredictable circumstances to come.

You are witnessing chaotic events in the world. Imagine yourself being in those events, surviving those events. Let them teach you what you would have to do, how you would have to prepare and think, what would be the wisest course of action. Let these terrible and unsettling events instruct you. Do not simply avoid them, or be horrified by them, or indulge in your own fears and fantasies. Instead, allow them to instruct you, for they are preparing you for the new world—a new world disorder, a new world instability.

Even geologically, the planet is becoming more unstable. It is affected by the events on the surface and by greater celestial bodies in the physical universe. Humanity has altered the circumstances of life through reckless abuse and overuse of the world's resources and by polluting the world's airs and waters and soils.

Now you are going to have to face the consequences and establish a new foundation, a sustainable foundation, for living in the world. This will require a change of heart, a change in thought, a change in activity so profound that most people do not even want to consider it, or they think that it is not possible.

But nature itself will teach you that it is not only possible but necessary. Nature is changing the terms of engagement in the world. You cannot see these new terms specifically in this moment, but Knowledge is already responding—Knowledge within you, Knowledge within others.

As you begin to enter the times of great instability, you will see people acting very foolishly and proclaiming many things. Many will say it is all temporary. Everything will be fine as soon as certain things are brought back in order. You will hear people say, "Do not worry. Nations will rebuild." You will hear many things said—great proclamations, optimistic proclamations, or others saying that it will be total catastrophe and everything will collapse.

But neither of these are true. The new world will be unstable and unpredictable, but humanity's experience in the world is not over. And in fact, the changing circumstances of your life give you the greatest possible opportunity to establish human unity in the world—cooperation built now of necessity, required to survive and to establish an orderly world in the face of great change.

Do not be in denial. Do not run away. Do not think that technology or governments are going to solve all of this for you. For you must become keen and clear and strong to recognize what is coming over the horizon and to prepare your life, not driven by fear and desperation, but by clarity and wisdom.

You are in the world to serve, so running away and hiding is not the answer. Believing in technology is not the answer. Believing in governance is not the answer. For everything will be vulnerable now.

It will take a thousand solutions for humanity to adapt to the new world. You do not have all of these solutions even in your mind yet. Humanity has not found them all yet, and those it has discovered have not been fully implemented yet.

But at the source and center of this is the power and the presence of Knowledge within you and within each person. Without this Knowledge, humanity will act foolishly. It will be complacent. And when it can no longer be complacent, it will panic and be desperate and destructive, further deteriorating the world, further wasting the critical resources that humanity will need into the future.

You will have to get beyond your fear to a place of greater clarity, certainty and strength. This means you are connected to Knowledge, for Knowledge is the only part of you that has this clarity and this strength. It is the only part of you that can see clearly and hear the truth in others and see the truth in the changing circumstances of the world.

The world is giving you signs, but can you respond? Can you see the signs? Will you spend time with the signs? And if they require action on your part, will you take this action, regardless of what other people are thinking, saying or doing? Will you allow your life to be guided by a greater power, greater than your intellect and understanding?

This is not a passive attitude. It is one of the greatest activity, keenness and discernment. God is not going to take care of you, but

God will guide you to take care of yourself and other people. God is not going to give you endless miracles to pad and secure your way.

You are going to have to climb this mountain. But God will teach you why you must climb; where you must climb; who can go with you and who cannot; what to take and what to leave behind; what to see, what to hear and what to know.

People become helpless, and then they want miracles from God because they have no strength. They have no clarity. Their relationships are weak and cannot support a greater strength within them.

In society, you will certainly have to take care of the elderly, the sick and the very young. But everyone else must rise to this great occasion. It is not simply for one great individual—an emancipator, a great spiritual figure, a great political figure, a great leader. No, not in the face of the Great Waves of change. You must strengthen the people, and the people must find the source of their strength, which is the power and the presence of Knowledge.

So while there are a thousand solutions and activities and endeavors that must be created and sustained, there is the source and center of your life. For everything that happens is a product of human beings, individuals, making decisions. The quality of those decisions and the wisdom of those decisions are determined by what informs them.

Are people guided by Knowledge or simply swayed by the political and social forces around them? Are decisions made merely out of expediency and for immediate profit, or are they engaged with the future in mind—the future well-being of humanity?

At this moment, people are selling their children's future away. They are creating a nightmarish future for their children by the way that they live and what they consume and what they believe and assume to be true, based upon their own habits and personal preference.

Who can see this? Who can know this? We are speaking of what is known, not what people want. People are guided by desire and fear, but the power of Knowledge is greater and more certain. The outcome of decisions based upon this will have a lasting impact, both now and into the future.

You cannot live only for the moment now. Snap out of that dream. It is a fool's paradise. You must live in the moment and prepare for the future all at once. This is what the birds and the beasts do. This is what you as an intelligent creature on Earth must do.

The world has changed, but people have not changed with it. You are entering a time of planetary instability, and this instability will grow. How are you going to recognize this, prepare for this and adapt to this?

Your intellect cannot answer these questions. No one can answer these questions completely. Even the wisest and most well informed cannot answer these questions completely. That is why the power of Knowledge is so critically important to you and to your family and to the world.

Humanity has run out of answers. It can only respond to catastrophe now. It is not prepared for the future. It has very little time. Whatever can be done should be done, but most people are still living in the dream of yesterday. They are still living in a world that no longer exists. Their expectations, their desires and demands are things that may not be met in the new world.

This can be seen in this moment—in a moment of great sobriety, a moment of great disappointment, a moment of true honesty and clarity within oneself.

Look upon the world, then, to see what it can show you and teach you about how you are going to build a greater stability in your life. Recognize that God's Revelation—the New Message for humanity— is what is being sent into the world to prepare humanity for the great change that is coming to the world and for its encounter with intelligent life in the universe.

Humanity's growing instability will call others from the universe around you to exploit the situation for themselves. They will come under the guise of being spiritually enlightened, to be great emancipators, to be true environmentalists. Whatever you want and expect, they will create this façade. Their technology will impress you, and their words will speak to your hidden desires and your hidden fears.

But no one is going to come and save humanity, and those who claim to be here for this purpose are here to take advantage of the situation. They are clever and cunning. They know what you are facing, for all intelligent life in their own home worlds had to face a decline in their environments. It is a prospect that few have been able to escape in the history of the universe.

How will humanity respond? How will you respond? How are you responding at this moment to the growing calamities and catastrophes around the world? Are you even looking? Are you paying attention?

If not, you are missing the signs and the instruction that the world is providing for you right now. It is preparing you for the Great Waves of change. But if your mind is not paying attention; if your thoughts are elsewhere; if you are overcome by anxiety, fearfulness and speculation, then you are not paying attention, you see. You are not looking and listening with a clear and objective mind.

Social upheaval, revolution, wars over resource acquisition, natural disasters, economic instability, nations falling into debt and financial collapse—this is all part of your future, you see. But you must look to see and listen. Listen to the outer world and listen to the inner world. And take the Steps to Knowledge.

This is how God is going to save you, not only from difficult and unpredictable circumstances. This is how God is going to save you from your own personal failure to respond to the greater purpose and calling of your life.

It is no accident that you are here in these times, facing these circumstances. It is not just a big inconvenience for you. It is the purpose of your life to call you out of your meaningless pursuit for self-satisfaction and pleasure, power and wealth, into a greater service and participation in the world.

It is only here that you will find your truly meaningful and sustainable relationships. It is here that your life will begin to make sense to you and your own individual nature will make sense because it has a real application in the world.

Here you escape the dreadful ambivalence and confusion of the past, and your past mistakes begin to serve you to build wisdom and clarity and to convince you that you cannot be successful in life without the power of Knowledge to guide you—a power and presence you have ignored in the past, a power and presence you were not aware of in the past.

There are no excuses now for failing. Not everyone will survive the Great Waves of change. You cannot alter this now. You can only mitigate it and adapt to it.

You cannot undo centuries of abuse and destruction to your natural environment and the misuse of your natural inheritance, living in this beautiful and magnificent world.

You cannot make these things go away. You cannot wish them away. You cannot pretend, and if you do so, you are failing to respond. You are failing to allow the situation to make you stronger, clearer and more honest with yourself and with others.

You were sent into the world to be in a planet that is becoming increasingly unstable, with an uncertain future and outcome. Can you face this? Where will you find the strength, the courage and the intention to face this—now when you have time to prepare your life; now when you have time to alert others; now when you have a period, a grace period, if you will, to prepare your outer life and to gain a connection with the source and center of your strength and certainty?

The choices here are clear, and their consequences are immense. The future prospects of humanity are being decided today and in the months and years to come. This is not a possibility. This is not one possible scenario. This is it. You rise or you fall. You respond or are overtaken. You prepare or your life is dashed.

The Great Waves will overcome the seeming strength of your cities, your economies and your political structures. You are seeing this in the world today. The evidence is there if you will look with clear eyes, without projecting your preferences, your ideology or your fear.

It is remarkable that most people's desires and ideology are based upon fear—the fear of not having, the fear of losing, the fear of death, the fear of deprivation, the fear of social rejection, the fear of being out of control, the fear of not knowing what to do in the face of danger.

Underlying humanity's great idealism and desires for its future—providence, wealth and affluence—is this fear. It is like the undercurrent—pulling, directing, moving people around.

The counterpoint to this is the power and presence of Knowledge. This is God's answer to a struggling humanity. It is the source of all true creation. It is the source of the desire to serve and to give, to produce and to create for the benefit of others as well as yourself. It is the source of all true and beneficial motivations.

Therefore, it is not merely a change in your thinking or behavior or habits. It is a change at the very source of what you listen to within yourself and what informs your decisions, what guides your actions, what enables you to see and what disables you from seeing. It is fundamental, you see.

You do not know how to prepare for planetary instability. But God knows how to prepare. God knows how to prepare you as an individual. God knows how to prepare the world. But God is not simply going to come and take over the planet. God is going to instruct people from the inside out.

God has given a New Revelation to tell you what is coming over the horizon, to teach you how to engage with intelligent life in the world with wisdom and clarity. God is going to teach you where to find the source and center of your power, and how to relate constructively and purposefully with others. God is going to provide the antidote to the undercurrent of fear that is driving individuals, communities and nations.

Life will become more difficult now, for almost everyone and eventually for everyone. Those who profit today may be the great losers in the future.

Yet this is a time of great calling, a time when Knowledge will emerge within you, the time of Revelation when God will speak again and provide humanity what it needs, what it cannot provide and see and know for itself.

It is the greatest time in human history, and you are here. You were chosen to come. You are fortunate in this regard, regardless of your outer circumstances. But you must hear the calling and feel the calling. Or you will shrink and decline in the face of the Great Waves of change.

Your questions, your issues, your denial, your frustrations—they do not matter, you see. They are not so important now. You have greater things to attend to. You have your life to bring in order and to reconsider and to redirect. You have your relationships to determine who has the strength to help you and who is holding you back. You have your own work and outer circumstances to consider whether these will be able to survive the Great Waves of change. You have your children's welfare. You have your aging parents perhaps to consider. You have many things to look at.

But you must look with clear eyes now. You cannot be driven by fear and desperation, or you will not see. You will not hear. And you will not know.

God has given you the eyes to see and the ears to hear, but this must be guided by Knowledge. Your intellect must be guided by Knowledge. Your life must be guided by Knowledge—now more than ever.

As circumstances become more difficult and the world grows darker, this is the time for Knowledge to emerge. This is the time of Revelation. This is the point where the future and the destiny of humanity is decided and determined, by the decisions made by individuals and the decisions made by you.

Accept your fate. Accept your calling. Accept the changing circumstances of the world. And then you can begin to build and to reconsider, to dismantle that which is weak and to build that which is strong, to alter the course of your life and to be a source of strength and direction for others.

What can you give to others? Beyond feeding them and giving them shelter, if that is their need in the moment, your greatest gift is to encourage them to take the Steps to Knowledge. For more than anything else, this will determine if they can face, prepare and respond to the great change that is coming to the world. Lead them to the source of their strength. And demonstrate this strength in your life and in your activities and in your outlook upon the world.

Then the disasters of the future will be the great calling for humanity to wake up and to grow up, to cooperate and to begin to use this world beneficially and sustainably so that you may have a future and so that your children may thrive and bring their gifts into the world.

CHAPTER 8

THE BATTLEGROUND

As revealed to
Marshall Vian Summers
on June 18, 2013
in Boulder, Colorado

You must speak out against war. It is never justified. It is errors compounded. It is failure compounded.

The incentive to go to war over resources, territorial control and overcoming a perceived enemy will be so great in the future when the resources of the world will diminish and economic difficulties will arise here, there and everywhere. It will be a great trial for humanity.

It is a challenge because humanity must become united in the face of the universe, a Greater Community of intelligent life. It must become united to utilize the resources of the world sufficiently and successfully to avoid ongoing competition, conflict and war. It will be a great trial for humanity.

People will feel threatened. They will take sides. They will believe others who take sides. When people are governed by fear, they take sides. When people are governed by anger or resentment, they take sides blindly, foolishly. They will be told who the enemy is, and they will believe what they are told. It will be a great trial for humanity. A trial is a test as well as a proving ground for what is true, what is just and what is honest.

There will either be cooperation or there will be conflict and war. The choices become much more simple and direct here. You cannot have it both ways. You cannot overcome another and establish the peace at the same time. You cannot suppress another people or even the people of your own nation and think you are maintaining justice, order and peace, for you are merely denying and resisting that which must come forward. But what must come forward is not simply revenge or hostility or the settling of scores.

You must be guided by a greater power within the people, the power that God has put there for all the peoples of the world, for all the religions of the world. Even for those who have no religion, it is there.

This power will see beyond division. It will see beyond complexity. It will see beyond the settling of scores to establish a cooperating reality based upon necessity and not merely high ideals and based upon the fundamental needs of people and what can assure that those needs will be sufficiently met.

God's New Revelation speaks of this greater power within the individual, speaks of it with such great emphasis, for it is the most important thing. Without this, you will be governed by fear, desire and the persuasions of others. You will side with your group, with your tribe, with your culture and maybe even your nation, or some force or faction within your nation. You will be blinded by their ideology, and you will believe because you will be so frightened that you will want to believe in something you can adhere to. You will not want to be alone, so you will associate with those who seem to be powerful and determined.

Thus, whole nations are corralled into war. Thus, people are cast into opposing forces, not even understanding what the conflicts are really about, not really understanding what they are doing and what they are supporting.

Radical forces, radical voices, will gain the world's attention as has been the case because that is what people want to listen to. They do not want moderation. They do not want restraint. They do not want diplomacy. They want to take what they think is theirs, prevent someone else from taking what they think is theirs or getting what is left as the world diminishes and declines. It is such a desperate situation in a world where humanity is so fractured and so divided.

You must overcome this, you see, but you must begin with yourself, for you are fractured and divided internally. You are given to radical persuasions. You tend to avoid that which you cannot face or try to put simple solutions on circumstances that are really more difficult to comprehend and to understand.

Look at your own tendencies. Look where your mind goes facing grave uncertainty and the prospect of war and conflict. Look how you take sides automatically or assume beliefs without ever really thinking or taking the time to understand a situation more deeply and more thoroughly which would give you pause and restrain you from coming to premature conclusions.

God has given you the great power to see, to know and to act with certainty. But to follow this, you have to step away from all the other seductions, directives and tendencies of your mind. If people will not do this, they will fall into ranks. They will become partisans in a splintering and disintegrating situation.

The battle lines are being drawn. Nations are vying for positions of control. Many who lead these nations understand the great change that is coming to the world. They want to have as strong a position as possible, to control access to resources as much as possible, to assure their security as much as possible. So they will vie for control and compete with others for control. But none of them understand the greater threat in the world, the threat of intervention from beyond the world that will seek to use human conflict, human ignorance and human ambition to its own ends.

The great understanding that humanity must have is not being adopted sufficiently, so God has given a New Message for the world—a message of warning, a message of power, a message of grace, a message of great hope. But this great hope can only be fulfilled if a sufficient number of people can receive the Revelation.

Many parts of the world are facing restrictions in food and water, for nature has been violated and the world's natural balance has been upset. Now the whole world will be facing violent weather, destroying much of the world's food production it will, and with it, the stability of nations, particularly the poorer nations of the world. While the stronger nations vie for position, struggling with each other, using poorer nations as their battleground, the poorer nations of the world will suffer and decline.

How much war will be waged, and how many lives will be ruined and lost? How much land will be destroyed? How many cities will be devastated? How much tragedy will have to occur before enough people come to their senses and realize their problem is not with one another? Their problem is with the world—their stability in the world itself, their stability within a Greater Community of life in which humanity has always lived and with which it must now learn to contend.

Who will guide humanity? What can God offer to humanity under such a grave and critical situation: the waste to the world of things that cannot be wasted, of land and infrastructure, of people and talents and abilities?

Nothing can be wasted in this new world, this world of greater demands, this world that will require human unity and cooperation at a level never seen before, not because everyone agrees ideologically, but because of sheer necessity itself, and because humanity is facing adversity and Intervention from the universe around it, functioning surreptitiously in the world, using the powers of deception and persuasion, casting nation against nation and people against people, discouraging entire populations so they will lose faith in their leaders and seek to be guided and governed by powers they do not understand.

This is the battleground. You either ruin what you have left and cast humanity into a much more grave and dire set of circumstances in the future, or people begin to come to their senses to realize that everything is at stake. No nation will prevail if the world declines too far, if too much is lost. No one's affluence will be safe and secure in a situation like this.

So what will prevail—wisdom, dignity and common sense, or anger, resentment and revenge? This is the great battleground. Not over territory, but over what will prevail in the minds and hearts of people. How many will have to die and suffer and be cruelly crippled before humanity can see what it must choose and commit itself to this path of resolution?

The religions of the world are divided and contentious even within themselves. Too often they have become partisans in the great struggles for power and dominance that have been waged throughout time and history. What is the guiding light there?

Not everyone will become a Christian. Not everyone will become a Muslim. Not everyone can become a Jew. And not everyone can follow any faith tradition or ideology. And yet many seek to dominate the world with their views and their religions. They too are sowing the seeds of war and conflict and mindless destruction upon the world.

That is why God has spoken again—not to condemn them but to offer a new way that does not require a strict ideology, that does not require that you repudiate another or another's group or nation, does not require that you believe in one hero.

You are standing on the battleground. It is here you will either build a new and more equitable and united future for the human family, or you will destroy yourselves—group by group, nation by nation—only to be exploited by those from beyond, who will seek to use you and direct you in your state of weakness, failure and decline.

If you knew the great hazards facing humanity, war would stop tomorrow. It would simply not be an option. If you knew what humanity will have to deal with and face, there would be little contention between nations.

This is the great trial, you see. Can humanity emerge from this great threshold intact, with a greater resolution, unity and strength? Or will it simply disintegrate and destroy itself in the face of what it has created in a world that has been exploited, wasting its precious resources on conflict, wasting its opportunity to establish a greater union here on Earth? And what kind of union will that be? Will that be a free union or will that be an oppressed state? The universe is full of technological, oppressed states.

Whatever the union is, you will have to have a union to survive in the Greater Community. You cannot be a set of warring tribes. You cannot be destroying the wealth and splendor and resources of the world over your ridiculous issues with one another. For pride, arrogance, power or advantage, you will destroy what is left. And then you will face a set of circumstances the human family as a whole has never had to face before—how to survive in a decimated world, how to survive in a climate that is out of control, a climate that has lost its natural stability because of human pollution and abuse.

It will take everything you have—your science, your ingenuity, your technology, human will and power just to survive in this world. And your ability to do so will determine what happens on this battleground and what this trial produces.

It is easy to go to war. It is more difficult to establish a union. It is easy to fall apart because that is what people do when they are weak and confused. It is more difficult to stand firm and maintain your strength and determination in times of great change and uncertainty. It is easy to attack another. It is more difficult to establish an agreement between you that is mutually supported.

Take the easy way, and you will face hardships that have never been known to the human family as a whole. And the world your children will have to live in, and their children, will be far more difficult and dangerous than what you face today.

They will bless you or curse you for what you have done in these times—this one great opportunity in this era to establish a greater unity, to prepare for a new world and reality, and to prepare for a Greater Community of intelligent life in the universe; this time of Revelation when God has spoken again to all the peoples of the world, to all the nations and all the religions of the world, to give them this greater perspective and this greater power and this greater opportunity that will be utterly wasted if humanity continues in its destructive and ignorant ways.

People of the world, hear the Voice of Heaven. And those who would wage war, particularly the religious who claim to be religious, Heaven will not look upon you favorably, for you are leading humanity into travail and far greater danger and difficulty.

What will prevail—human strength and wisdom, or human weakness and indolence? What will prevail? What must be built carefully over time, or what is expedient in the moment? What will prevail in you? You can always blame others and speak about humanity in generalities, but what about you? Where will your mind go? What position will you take? What will you support? You cannot merely look out for yourself, for that is destructive. You must consider how everyone can have greater stability and encouragement.

This is a challenge not only for leaders of nations, or great thinkers, or philosophers, or theologians. It is a challenge for each person who sees that they must really consider what is happening in the world and what they can do to contribute to a positive and constructive outcome.

Like it or not, believe it or not, you are standing on the battleground right now—an economic battleground, a political battleground, a military battleground, a battleground even within yourself over what you will follow and what you will stand for at a time of greater uncertainty and upheaval in the world.

God has spoken again to all the peoples of the world to give them strength, courage and dignity and a pathway out of confusion, danger and self-destruction. But who will listen to this and not merely defend their old ideas or their position, or speak for their own group, or protect their self-interest? Those who have taken sides and those who will take sides, can you hear God speaking to you again—admonishing you, correcting you, honoring you and directing you?

In the next twenty years, if the great remaining resources are squandered, the world will be poor, poorer than you can imagine. Humanity may survive, but in a very much declined state. It is not a world where anyone really benefits. Even those few who have wealth will be surrounded by those who do not. Their position will not be sustainable.

This is the seriousness of these times. This is the importance of your life. You did not merely come here to be a locust upon the land and consume everything in sight, as the wealthy do so often. You came here to give something unique and special to a world in need.

Do not complain about the world, for this is the world that will offer you redemption if you can understand it and respond to it correctly.

Do not condemn yourself, for you know not of your greater purpose, your greater origin and your greater destiny.

Each one of you is important. Each one of you has gifts for the world—gifts that you cannot ascertain from your own desires and preferences, but what must be called out of you by the circumstances of the world, often by circumstances you might choose to avoid or have avoided in the past. This is what brings greatness out of people, not their pathetic little wishes and obsessions and fantasies.

You are standing on the battleground, determining the future and the fate of humanity. Each one of you and all of you will contribute to this in one way or the other. There is no neutral ground. You cannot stand apart and think of yourself as above and beyond all this, for this is the world you have come to serve. And Knowledge, the greater power that God has given you, is determined and focused on you finding this service and fulfilling it here.

It is okay that things are not perfect. Stop complaining about this. When people are in danger, they do the greatest things. When there is the greatest need, the greatest creations are made. When the greatest needs prevail, the greatest inventions come forward. You are not made great by pleasure and indolence, but by contribution and selfless giving of yourself and life and resources.

Do not think your belief in a great savior is going to save you unless you can give to the world what you came to give. Do not think that your religious ideology is going to set you above and beyond everyone else. For if you cannot contribute to human unity and cooperation with peoples from different nations and religions, then you are working against the welfare and well-being of humanity, no matter what you believe or what your hero or heroine might be.

Heaven looks upon those who can contribute to human unity, cooperation and adaptation to a new world and to a Greater Community of life. For your isolation in the universe is over, and you will never have it again. The time has come for humanity to contend with this, and there is no running away from this reality.

It is what is necessary that is important. It is what must be that is important. It is courage, purpose and destiny that are important. Do not think your intellectual position is significant. It is only what you give and do not give, what you support and do not support that makes any difference to the outcome for your life and destiny, and for the well-being of the world. Here there must be great humility and great service, or you will not understand why you are here, what you must do and what the world is calling from you and requiring of you.

You are on the battleground. There is no hiding. There is no running away. There is no living in fantasy. There is no thinking that you are special and unique because of anything.

The world is declining. Humanity is sowing the seeds of future conflict. War is raging here, there and everywhere. The climate is unstable. Economies are contracting. You must participate in this greater reality and serve wherever your true service can be rendered. In this, you will know Heaven, and Heaven will know you, regardless of your religious beliefs.

For you are at the dawning of a new era of human unity and cooperation, or a new era of human self-destruction. The outcome will be determined upon the battleground—the battleground upon which you stand today.

CHAPTER 9

BUILDING GLOBAL SECURITY

As revealed to
Marshall Vian Summers
on February 14, 2009
in Boulder, Colorado

Humanity is moving in a dangerous direction now, heedless of the warning signs that it is overreaching what the world can provide, living in the moment, thinking only of the near term.

Humanity is entering dangerous waters, unknown territory, where it will have to face a world in decline—a world of declining resources, a world of environmental disruption, a world of violent weather, a world of diminishing food production, a world of greater economic hardship and instability, a world that will in many places strip away the thin veneer of civilization, setting people in competition with one another.

This threshold, which is so great, has been coming for a long time. For those who have the eyes to see, they can anticipate this. It represents a fundamental imbalance between man and nature, a fundamental imbalance within man and man's own nature, as well as humanity's relationship with the world itself.

People are preoccupied with their own needs and their own desires. So many people want God in the universe to provide more, more than they need, to provide the burden of wealth and great ownership of things, while so many others need the very basic things of life.

Humanity seems incapable of correcting itself. While there are very aware individuals who are working on various aspects of humanity's problems and needs, nations of people and leaders of nations and religions seem incapable of grasping the situation as it really is and as it will be if humanity does not alter its course.

The answers seem so elusive, and the cost of correction seems so great, but the very principles upon which people function, the very foundation of people's thoughts and expectations, will over time have to change and to adapt to a declining world. What a great change this would be.

Humanity is completing its tribal existence in the world. It has been in this process for a very long time. It is now having to face the reality of living as a one-world community.

Nations will still be nations. Competition will still exist between them. There will still be friction and conflicts, conflicts of interest and so forth. But increasingly people will have to face a global reality, and not just a local or regional reality.

If there is a drought in one region of the world, the cost of food goes up halfway around the world. If there is financial corruption in one place, it can change the financial reality of millions and millions of people far, far away.

It is not enough to just be concerned with national security. Now you will have to be concerned with global security.

You are facing competition from the universe around you. Resource explorers, economic collectives are infiltrating the world in small groups—seeking to turn the tide of humanity's actions to their advantage through persuasion and deception, seeking to gain strength, seeking to turn individuals towards them and away from human leadership.

But who can see this amongst the preoccupied? They do not even know what is happening in their own homes. They do not know what is happening in their own bodies concerning their health. They are unaware of the problems that are growing and expanding in their own communities to a large extent.

Perhaps they have an awareness of one area of difficulty, but people are losing their ability to see the bigger picture, so involved they are in specific areas alone. So those who are concentrated on the financial world have no idea what is happening in the natural world, and vice versa. So people do not have an overview. And, as a result, they cannot see what is coming over the horizon, so focused they are on their one particular area of interest or profession.

So humanity is entering this grave and difficult time—unprepared, thinking only of the near term, thinking that everything is correct and will be like the past, the very recent past, of course. They cannot see the bigger picture. They cannot see that civilization is imperiled. They are fighting fires today, but they do not see what is creating the fires of tomorrow and the days to come.

So very tepid solutions are proposed, and even these can be resisted. No one wants to give up anything unless everyone makes sacrifices. And so the fingers are pointed at each other, but no one is saying, "Really, this is what we must do." And those who do say these things are ignored, or vilified, or repudiated. So the visionaries are denied.

The change in how the wealthy nations will have to live will be so significant, driven now by necessity. But people still think that their lifestyle is non-negotiable, that these changes cannot happen, and they will fight them.

So now the world is losing its security. By the time that humanity deals even with the changing climate, it will be too late given its present course of action.

Economic hardship is now gripping the world because humanity has overspent even its own self-created wealth, as well as its natural inheritance. It has not saved for the future. It has not planned for the future. It has not provisioned for the future. And the future is coming relentlessly.

For the individual, the temptation is to give up, or to become enraged, or to attack your neighbors or other nations or leaders. But everyone has been a part of this problem. People have benefited greatly from the overuse of the world, and they will resist having to change course now to any really meaningful degree.

The solutions will have to be wrought by individuals and small groups. The innovation will have to happen at the very fundamental levels of society, and there will have to be many of them.

But you are working against time now. Time is of the essence. A decade wasted will have great bearing on the future prospects and options available to the world.

So for the individual, the pathway is to follow Knowledge, the deeper Intelligence that God has placed within you—to follow this, and to learn to distinguish it from the other forces and persuasions in your mind. And how can this be done, one would ask? It seems so impossible, so difficult.

A preparation has been sent into the world from the Creator of all life to prepare the individual, and guidelines have been sent to prepare the nations. A warning is being sounded about the Great Waves of change coming to the world and humanity's destined encounter with a Greater Community of intelligent life in the universe.

The problem has been clarified. The reality has been made clear. The danger has been brought forth. And humanity's ability to respond and to create and to change course has been amplified and encouraged.

How to bring about these great changes will have to involve the talents of many people, and can be difficult to discern and work out, but the direction must be clear. It is not enough to just be cynical and think, "Well, that will never happen," or think you are going to go back to some previous era that seemed to be untroubled by these things.

It seems remarkably difficult for people with vested interests to see the situation clearly and to realize the depth and gravity of the great change that is coming now. So foolishness persists. People argue endlessly over details. They underestimate the great change that is coming. They do not recognize how they must change their lives and expectations. They do not see that all of civilization is so greatly imperiled—imperiled by risk of collapse within and by intervention from without.

So the recklessness continues. The wealthy are lost in their indulgences. The poor become more desperate, and their numbers are growing. The resources of the world are not being planned and preserved and wisely used and cultivated.

Despite people's optimism and excuses, self-denial and avoidance, and all the other tendencies that people can have in the face of great change, there is a deep anxiety running through the minds and the hearts of people everywhere. They sense that great difficulty is coming, but still they argue and bicker over their issues: the Middle East, their economic situation, resenting other nations, denying other peoples. They continue the same behaviors, the same tendencies, but beneath all this there is a great anxiety. That anxiety is telling you something. It is not merely a lack of optimism. It is a response beyond the reach of the intellect and all of its machinations and self-deceptions.

So ultimately you come to a place as an individual where you say, "What is the truth and what must I do?" That is the beginning of a deeper response and a greater responsibility if it can be honored and followed.

The New Revelation from God calls upon individuals to ask these questions repeatedly—not to gain simple, immediate answers but to live with the questions so that the answers can reveal themselves slowly and incrementally, step by step over time.

God has given a great warning as to what humanity is really facing— a warning that goes far beyond what the vast majority of people are aware of, or even willing to see and know.

A Revelation that is clear is not a matter of perspective. It is not a matter of philosophy. It is not a matter of a school of thought or social conditioning or educational orientation or religious belief. It is a Revelation.

For the world is now imperiled. Human civilization's foundation is beginning to erode quickly. You are now facing problems of such an enormous magnitude that it will take global cooperation and adaptation to deal with them. It will not simply be a matter of a new technology or political resolutions.

It is like an emergency in the world. You are facing environmental decline. You are facing Intervention from the universe around you. Everyone should know about this. Everyone should be looking at this. The nations must prepare their peoples. There must be a greater reckoning, or the response will be too weak and too latent and too ineffectual.

If you do not understand the challenge, you will not see the need. If you do not see the need, you will not create the response. You will think the need is just an economic problem, or a political problem, or just a problem in human perception, a philosophical problem, an ideological problem, an emotional problem. And if someone spells out the reality, well, it seems so radical, so extreme, so negative, so fearful.

So people choose not to look. But the animals are looking. The birds are watching. Why is it that the intelligent race will not look, will not watch, will not respond, while the simple creatures are always watching, trying to discern change in their environment, trying to adapt to changing circumstances?

It is global security now that is the issue, so you must think like the people of the world within a Greater Community of intelligent life. Humanity is not highly regarded in this Greater Community—a warring set of tribes destroying a magnificent world that is of value to others. Who would not intervene for their own self-interest in this regard to preserve these resources and to use humanity as a workforce?

You think you are alone in the universe. You think that others cannot reach your shores. You think that intelligent life is rare in the vastness of space. What foolish projection is this?

You will have to defend the planet. You will have to establish your own rules of engagement with races visiting the world. You will have to limit human consumption in the world. You will have to limit human reproduction in the world. You will have to stabilize your population and do this in such a way that human freedom and the morality of your innate spirituality is not violated by this. It is a matter of survival now.

You cannot conquer the worlds around you beyond this solar system. Those worlds are owned by others who are far more powerful than you. You will have to live with what the world can provide. If you lose your self-sufficiency, you will be prone to seduction by others and you will become dependent upon them. And when that happens, human freedom and sovereignty will be lost in this world. You will have lost the most precious thing you have—given away blindly, mindlessly, foolishly, out of greed and necessity.

Deplete the world and you will accept whatever any other race will offer you because you will not have the power to decline. You cannot be like an adolescent: wild, irresponsible, unaccountable, immature.

Humanity will have to husband its resources now. Precious they are: water, food and energy. Eventually, humanity will have to face what every evolving nation in the universe has to face—to face the limits of their resources.

If you are to be a free race in the universe, you must be self-sufficient, you must be united, and you must be very discreet. No more broadcasting out into space all of your foolishness, your weakness, everything. To more mature nations in this region of space, you appear to be like wild children—reckless and destructive, greedy and ambitious, hardly trustworthy, vulnerable now to intervention and persuasion.

The corruption you are facing in the world today, the disruption of your economic systems, is just emblematic of humanity's problem in irresponsibility and immaturity. This is not merely a matter for leaders of nations; it is an awareness for the citizens of the world. They are much freer to see the truth. They are much less restrained by all the restraints that exist in the corridors of power.

You change the world by changing your life. You begin with your life. You do not just demonstrate for others. You change your life. You learn how to live differently. And if you are wise, you are guided by Knowledge, for God has already answered your questions and your needs. It is all contained within Knowledge. Only Knowledge will know how to navigate the difficult and uncertain waters ahead.

If you follow your intellect, you will simply be bound to the past—to past expectations and to past interpretations. You will become lost in a world of competing ideas and different theories.

Meanwhile, the foundation of civilization is eroding away. If humanity cannot feed its peoples, it will descend into chaos. If humanity cannot assure its future energy requirements, even on the fundamental level, things will descend into chaos. If wealth is squandered by the rich and the greedy, if resources are overspent, if the world is degraded, then you are facing a situation far more grave than any world war, than any human conflict that has ever existed here before. And what will happen to human freedom and creativity under such dire necessity?

If you prepare for the future, you will be able to ride the waves of change and benefit from them as well. If you do not prepare for what is coming, then it will overtake you and deprive you, for you did not see it coming.

This is already the lament of so many people today: They did not see it coming. Why? Because they were not looking; they were not listening; they were not paying attention. Obsessed with small problems, they missed the big ones. Concerned only with the details, they lost track of the greater direction of things.

There must be a change of heart here, or real change will not occur. There will be pronouncements of change, there will be promises of change, there will be declarations of change, there will be celebrations of change, but real change will not happen.

Those people who are choosing to live differently in the wealthy nations, they are promoting real change by demonstration. Those people who are taking care of the poor and depressed and deprived peoples of the world, they are promoting real change. Those people who are consuming less of the world, as a matter of moral and ethical principle, they are promoting real change. Those people who are committing themselves to what humanity will need in the future and not simply to the fashions and fantasies of humanity, they are part of real change.

Without this, the radical, political elements will govern the day and determine the fate of everyone. The minority extreme views will dominate the conversation, and everyone will be a victim to them.

The understanding here is very simple. Unite and you can succeed. Divided you will fail. If you cannot coexist, there will be no existence.

Religions of the world were initiated by the One God. There should be no competition between them; there should be no conflict between them. They are the different pathways to the Divine. They are not the exclusive truth of one organization or set of institutions.

This is a matter of necessity now, not simply preference. It cannot be the ideals of the elite. It has to be fundamental. It has to be part of the education of everyone if you are to have global security.

The Intervention that is happening today must become public so the people can prepare, so all eyes can be watching the skies for the protection of humanity.

Without this change of heart and approach, humanity will drive itself into chaos—into collapsing economies, collapsing nations, collapsing trade, collapsing relations between peoples, collapsing prospects, collapsing lives.

This is what God is revealing. It is not the perspective of an individual. It is not a school of thought. Do not be foolish in thinking this. You want to know what is coming? God has revealed it. You want to prevent chaos? God has revealed it. You want to know what to do? God has given you the clarity and the vision to begin the re-evaluation of your own life and circumstances. You want to know how happiness is achieved? Through service and contribution, through community and cooperation.

You could begin to put the rest of the puzzle together for yourself once you see what it really looks like, once you have a vision of what is coming and what humanity must do to preserve human freedom and human sovereignty in this world. You can fill in all the other spaces then because you know what the picture looks like. But without this reference point, the pieces seem to have no relationship with each other, and the puzzle seems to be too complex, too frustrating to deal with.

People project what they want, or what they are afraid of, but they cannot see clearly yet, except for a very few. It takes great courage to look, but you need this courage because your life depends upon it. The life of your children depends upon it. You look without hope, without fear, to see clearly what is coming and prepare for that.

Governments will seem incompetent, financial institutions too corrupt, too self-serving. So the vision must happen at the individual level at all echelons of society, in all societies. The conversation must change.

It is the gift of all human minds and hearts to address this great need for global security, and for the preservation of human freedom and sovereignty in this world, and for the well-being of all peoples in the world, and for the plans that must be made to secure the future and security of the world.

Time is of the essence. This is not merely an academic exercise. This is not merely something that you think about now and then. This is not something that is reserved for the specialists, or for the elites, or for the academic world. For [they are] as blind as any other group of people.

If you cannot see the picture clearly, then you will not know what is coming, and you will not prepare, and your life today will not be informed by what is coming over the horizon, and your decisions will be out of personal interest in the moment and will not be effective for the future.

Heed and receive the blessings of the Creator, the power of Revelation, the guidelines for preparation. The Lord of the universe is trying to save humanity from its own blindness and its own tendencies. Humanity can succeed if it can prepare, and it will prepare if it recognizes what it is facing.

You have the strength, you have the power, you have the inspiration if you can see clearly and respond to the power of guidance that God has placed within you.

This is not a time to seek personal fulfillment. This is not a time to indulge yourself in romances. It is not a time to lose yourself in your hobbies, your fantasies, your pleasures. For you are living at a time of great emergency. This will tell you what to do, and where to go, and who to meet, and where your gifts can come forward, and where your life can become meaningful, and where you can have the great satisfaction of contributing to a world in need. That is where happiness and fulfillment will be found.

You were born for these times. You are here to meet these problems. That is why you have come now. Your real nature and your real gifts are about this. Do not look at the great change that is coming as a massive inconvenience or a great tragedy alone. It is the calling. And your heart will respond even if your mind is in confusion.

This is the awareness that will turn your life into a path of true promise and accomplishment. It will temper your greed, your self-denial, your condemnation of others. It will be the antidote to ignorance and self-deception. And it will protect you against deception from any form, whether it be human or from the Greater Community itself.

This is your calling and your time. You were sent here for this. See this, and your path will become clearer, and a way will open up before you. You will ask a different set of questions and be concerned with a different set of ideas. And the world will not be this frightening place you are trying to avoid, but actually the arena for your success and your accomplishment.

CHAPTER 10

PREVENTING COLLAPSE AND THE WARS OF DESPERATION

As revealed to
Marshall Vian Summers
on January 2, 2009
in Boulder, Colorado

With the world's resources diminishing and ever-growing numbers of people drinking from a slowly shrinking well, the risk of competition, conflict and war is increasing. Groups and nations that are already in contention with one another will find it difficult to resist the temptation to claim those resources that they need for their own peoples.

As resources diminish, nations will become more protective of what they have. And there will be less available for nations around the world to purchase these resources—resources here, not merely industrial materials, but food, the availability of water, medicines, things that are fundamental to the well-being of people everywhere.

But while the risk of war is growing and the conditions of war are increasing, that does not mean that war is inevitable. It does not mean that you cannot stop it or mitigate it.

The changing conditions of the world are providing humanity with a fundamental requirement. And that is to conserve its resources, to protect its resources and to not overuse its resources. Yet that will require a great change from how people view these things today.

Today humanity is like the locust in the field, devouring everything in sight, assuming there will always be new fields. Some people even assume there will be new worlds to explore once the Earth has been depleted, but that approach is self-destructive and has no future.

You cannot go out in the universe to claim what you have destroyed here on Earth, for those resources are owned by others. And in most cases they are far more powerful than you. Besides, you will need to establish a greater wealth and stability to ever be able to leave this planet and to explore your surrounding environments.

The emphasis in the world is still on growth, on expansion. Whole economic systems are based upon growth and access to ever-greater amounts of resources. This cannot continue. That is why the change at hand is so monumental, so fundamental and far-reaching.

Humanity will have to enter a different kind of paradigm, a different kind of emphasis overall that will have to be on stability and security, for you have reached the limits of what growth can produce.

While there may be certain new industries that grow and expand, humanity's overall use of the world cannot grow. It will have to find new resources, of course. But the whole emphasis will have to change.

You will have to adapt to a changing world and to the Great Waves of change that are coming to the world—great changes in your environments and your climates, violent weather, the diminishing production of food, economic and political instability and crises.

This will require tremendous courage and change. But this change
cannot be accomplished through war, for war destroys resources for
everyone. And in that sense, war is ultimately self-destructive.

While this price could be postponed or could be offset in the past
because you always had a world requiring greater exploration and
new resources, you have now come to the threshold where the world
cannot provide much more for its growing human population. And
that is why the emphasis overall will have to change.

If humanity continues on its current trajectory, it will deplete the
world beyond restoration in forty years. And in the time in between,
you will face such calamitous instability, and even the collapse of
nations.

Do not think that technology alone will resolve these problems.
There must be a change of heart, a change in the way people live,
particularly amongst the wealthy nations—an emphasis on
simplicity, an emphasis on self-sufficiency.

As energy resources decline or become more unavailable, people will
have to become more regional and local in their emphasis, which
means their resources will have to come from sources that are closer
at hand. This is a complete change in emphasis for many nations in
the world today. This will be driven not by ethics or morality as much
as by absolute necessity.

Here war becomes unthinkable because it garners no real advantage.
War was always a fool's pursuit except in rare cases where one had to
defend one's nation against invading armies. But war for conquest of
resources now will produce consequences that are far more costly

than any benefits that can be achieved for any group or nation. This is a practical matter now as well as a moral and ethical issue.

People will have to use less and become more self-reliant. Overconsumption here is the engine of war, requiring your nation now to seek resources beyond its own lands, resources that it must acquire at any cost—generating intervention and deception and manipulation of other peoples and nations.

Yet this emphasis will not be given up easily. Perhaps humanity will have to face a series of tragic calamities in order to persuade it that it must change its approach and establish a different system and emphasis. Intelligent races change based upon recognition, and races that are exercising less intelligence learn based on tragic consequences.

Therefore, people must have greater vision here. They must look beyond tomorrow. They must look out into the future on the horizon of life to see what is really coming. They must have the courage and the determination to face times of change and great uncertainty. Continuing to emphasize growth and the wonders of technology will be self-defeating, as they are even today self-defeating.

Soils around the world will have to be rejuvenated, not by technology but by biological rejuvenation, or they will fail humanity's needs in the future.

Rivers will have to be cleaned up. Lakes will have to be cleaned up. Water is precious. It is precious in many places in the world and will become ever increasingly so all around the world as water resources become scarce in highly populated regions.

Food production will be interrupted and even destroyed in large regions due to violent and unpredictable weather. This is occurring already in many places, affecting the lives of people all around the world.

The great challenge for humanity here on Earth is how it will feed and care for its peoples. It will not be who can become rich and make money by doing nothing. That is a fool's paradise. And it is actually to your benefit that you are coming to the end of this great and foolish endeavor.

In essence now, besides the moral and ethical problems regarding human conflict, which are real and substantial, you simply cannot afford war. It will cost you too much. It will cost everyone too much. It has always cost everyone too much. Now you cannot afford it.

But that does not mean it cannot happen and will not happen if great effort is not exercised to prevent the conditions that will make war inevitable. If people are hungry, they will not be reasonable or rational or accommodating. If people are losing their forms of self-sufficiency, you cannot expect them to behave in an orderly, sensible or productive manner.

This is the great risk. This is the risk of war beyond the assertions of power by one nation over another, or by historical or religious differences or longstanding grievances between nations and groups. That will be a war of utter desperation, a war of terrible consequences, a war that would be very difficult to extinguish.

It is in this new world you are entering, a world in decline, that wars of desperation will become increasingly possible and can only be thwarted and prevented by the wise and ethical maintenance of resources and distribution of resources.

Eventually, humanity will have to find humane and ethical ways to limit its population. But you are not there yet. Eventually, humanity will have to change its entire relationship with the world. But you are not there yet. The emphasis here is practical, as well as moral and ethical.

The wealthy nations will have to encourage simplicity and self-sufficiency in an ever-increasing manner. Those who are wealthy will have to use their wealth to help other people in very direct and significant ways. Many luxuries will have to be set aside because the resources will be much more important to be used in other ways.

Instead of buying the new car or the beautiful jewelry, you support a village halfway around the world. Instead of the endless acquisitions of things you do not really need, you make sure that food is reaching the people who have the greatest need for it. Instead of this endless indulgence in one's personal beauty and health, your emphasis becomes helping people, feeding people, serving people who have the greatest needs.

In the future, there will have to be great emphasis on caring for the elderly, who will be much more vulnerable than they are today. The requirements for selfless activity, service to humanity, will be so overwhelming that this should consume the thoughts and the goals of the wealthy, particularly, but also [be] the emphasis for people everywhere.

You will have to earn enough money now to take care of other people, perhaps people you do not even know—those who are

vulnerable in your community, children without parents, elderly
people, people with disabilities. The government will not be able to
take care of all these people.

Take your vital energy and direct it here. Learn to grow food in
your backyard, in empty lots, everywhere you can, for food will be
precious in the future, more precious than it is today, more difficult
to acquire.

This has many positive benefits, bringing people together in
supporting people's constructive behavior as an antidote to personal
obsession and addiction. This can generate much greater humanity
and recognition between peoples. Here people's needs are all the
same. And they are authentic needs, not the indulgences of the rich
or the compulsive. These are essential needs. This brings people
together.

Governments will have to face the emphasis of taking care of their
own people instead of trying to exert influence or dominance over
other peoples and nations. If the needs of the people are simple,
governments can do this. But if the needs of the people are
overarching and complex, then the governments will have to try to
acquire resources by any means.

Here you must recognize there is a real difference between the
cessation of war and the establishment of peace. A peaceful society
requires peaceful minds. If minds are not at peace, if they are at
war—full of conflict and enmity and condemnation—all you can
hope for then is the cessation of war, the restraint of war.

Not everyone is going to be peaceful. And in times of great change
and uncertainty, people will be less peaceful, less accommodating

and in many cases less wise and compassionate. You cannot ask people to change and also ask them to be at peace. For change is difficult and upsetting. It involves risk. It exposes one's weakness and condemnation of others, one's prejudices and one's limitations.

That is why stability and security must become the emphasis. People can only become so insecure or so unstable before societies begin to break down, and social disorder begins to erupt, and groups turn against one another, and nations are pulled into greater and greater conflict—wars of desperation.

You are entering dangerous times now—uncertain times, a difficult time of adjustment for people everywhere, a time that will require greater human unity and cooperation. Here you, yourself, must become more accountable and responsible for how you live and for what you consume and what you do, what you give and what you take. You cannot simply defer to authority leaders or to government agencies. Everything you do must follow what you know to be right. That includes your role as a consumer.

Many people have high ideals and values, but they want to buy the cheapest things, always. They always want the bargain item, not realizing or wanting to recognize that these things come from the worst working conditions in the world. So while they espouse peace and harmony and well-being for people, they are supporting the most degrading industries, the worst human working conditions, the greatest human exploitation.

Everything you do now needs to be part of an ethical foundation. Everything you buy, everything you consume, everything that you use must be done with greater conscience and greater awareness.

PREVENTING COLLAPSE AND THE WARS OF DESPERATION

It is true today that there are many nations that are not self-sufficient in the production of food, in the availability of water and in the manufacture of essential goods. So trade between nations and interdependence between nations is a reality and cannot be undone.

But the emphasis of governments must change from trying to become dominant, from trying to threaten their neighbors, towards taking care of the essential needs of their peoples. While this seems obvious, it is not the case today.

Governments want to protect themselves more than their peoples. They want to assert power and influence. They want to support military actions in other nations. They want to support revolutions or terrorist organizations or uprisings and so forth. Some nations want to destroy other nations' economic fabric by importing cheap goods, thereby destroying the productivity of the people they are selling things to. The examples here are many. And this is leading to greater instability, greater uncertainty and greater tensions between peoples and nations. Instead of importing so many goods, people should be establishing these industries for themselves.

The problem with all nations becoming so interdependent is that when one falls, the others fall with them. Human civilization becomes more fragile and less resilient. So the balancing point here must be established from the reality of the world and the real condition of peoples around the world.

It is not enough for wealthy nations to simply give charity to nations that are in crisis, or where starvation is occurring. The wealthy nations will have to change their behavior, shift their values, become more responsible and accountable for how they live and for how they use the world.

Here there must be a revolution in thinking more than a revolution of arms—a greater sensitivity, a greater awareness, a greater responsibility for people. This is redeeming and this is necessary.

As the world is changing, you must change to adapt to it. As resources are declining, you must change to adapt to this. Here you must use everything carefully. There cannot be the amount of waste that exists today, profligate waste.

This is a sign of humanity's decadence and ignorance. It is a sign that humanity is not paying attention to the condition of the world and is not aware of its own vulnerability in this regard.

People think the world will just continue to provide endlessly for their ever-escalating set of needs and desires, like it is a cornucopia of wealth that just requires investment and expenditure. That is an old paradigm of thinking, an old way of looking at the world.

In a certain way, it was appropriate in history. But now humanity is becoming dangerously close to overusing the world to such an extent that you are changing the condition of the world itself. The world will not accommodate human habitation if this change is continued.

War is a failure. War is always a failure in human communication and human recognition. But wars of desperation are a failure at a much greater level, a kind of failure that cannot really be undone.

For once you are driven to desperation, then your options are few. You have already passed the point at which mitigation can take place. You have already driven yourself to the point of desperation. And it is in this environment that humanity's greatest weaknesses and greatest liabilities come into play.

PREVENTING COLLAPSE AND THE WARS OF
DESPERATION

It is important that governments everywhere in the world begin to educate their peoples about the changing condition of the world and about the Great Waves of change that are coming to the world, and how humanity must adapt to these changes before the real limitations are placed upon the people. People can adapt to change if they are aware of it and can prepare for it and have time to prepare for it. But they need this time. They need this preparation. To not inform peoples of what is coming, that is irresponsible and unconscionable.

This is a Message for all of humanity. It comes from the Creator of all life. It is a gift of profound love and respect. But it also contains a warning and a revelation of what is coming over the horizon.

Humanity is borrowing from its future now. It is spending its future resources. It is spending its natural endowment at such a rate that it is heading towards depletion and collapse.

If you cannot see this, then you are not looking. If you think that technology alone will resolve all of these problems, then you are not seeing the limits of technology and the dangers of deprivation. If you cannot see that the world is a shrinking well, then you will not recognize the consequences of your actions or the future that you are heading into—a future that you will not be able to avoid, a future that will affect everyone.

Stability and security cannot be used by tyrants to oppress the peoples. There cannot be an excuse to destroy freedom and self-expression. But it is a fundamental reality that you must face as part of the natural world and as a citizen of human civilization. This recognition is fundamental.

Many people cannot see this because they are so jaded in their political viewpoint. They are so distrustful of other people. They are so condemning of human leaders and institutions that they are blinded to the very natural circumstances that give them life, that promise them life for the future. Here humanity is depending upon a set of assumptions that are no longer valid and that cannot be sustained.

God has given each person a deeper Intelligence, the greater power of Knowledge, an Intelligence that is not filled with enmity and judgment or false assumptions; an Intelligence that is here to protect you, to guide you and to lead you to a greater life in service to the world.

It is at this deeper level that you will find your humanity, your compassion and your strength. It is at this deeper level that you will come to recognize that these words that We speak are true and cannot be denied without putting yourself and your community and nation at grave risk.

This is not a message of fear. This is a message of love and respect and concern. Do not misinterpret this, or you will not recognize the gift of wisdom that this really is and how it will strengthen you and renew your life.

Great change in the world will require great change in human awareness, in human thinking, in human beliefs and assumptions. Do not pray to God thinking God will give you ever-greater abundance, for God has given you this world and one another. If you cannot find the splendor there, if you cannot use these resources and this wealth responsibly, in such a way that your children and their children will have a future, then do not ask God for anything else. If

you use up your natural inheritance, then do not think that God or
some race from another world will come to save you.

You are entering the era of human responsibility and cooperation.
You must be able to respond. That is response-ability, human
responsibility and cooperation, rather than the individual quest for
wealth and dominance.

The world is changing, and you must change with it. You must adapt
to it and hope that it does not adapt to you beyond what can sustain
humanity in the future. It is this recognition and this power of
Knowledge that will give you the clarity and the certainty and the
understanding that you will need to proceed and to navigate the
difficult times ahead.

Here you will find the strength to reconsider your life in a deep
evaluation. Here you will see how you can be of service to others,
and how you can be part of the great and necessary change that must
occur, particularly amongst the wealthy nations where people have
the freedom to redirect their lives and to change their circumstances.

You will find your strength in Knowledge. You will find your
direction at the level of Knowledge. You will find your humanity
and the humanity of others at the level of Knowledge. You will want
others to succeed so that you can succeed. You will want others to
be stable so that you can be stable. You will want others to have
their needs met so you do not have to struggle with them and fight
with them over who will survive and who will not survive. Here you
will see that you and others must not become desperate. That is the
great danger, and that is a great hazard.

The power for you to see this and know this and to bring this awareness into the world is with you now. Perhaps it is not reflected in your thoughts, beliefs and attitudes, but it is fundamental to the deeper Knowledge that God has given you, which has not been changed and corrupted by the world.

It is this power that you must now have to find your way and to find the courage, the strength and the determination you will need as an individual to enter a new world and to find success and fulfillment there.

CHAPTER 11

THE GREAT TRANSITION

As revealed to
Marshall Vian Summers
on March 1, 2011
in Boulder, Colorado

Humanity will have to unite in the future to sustain and to secure human civilization. There will have to be a greater unity and cooperation, or nations will fail, and other nations will fail, and societies will begin to break down.

This is the future, the next great stage of human evolution and development. The last 2000 years was the creation of human civilization, the emergence from tribal societies into greater societies. It has been a difficult and often tragic process, but necessary because this is evolution for humanity as it is for all races in the universe, in the Greater Community of life of which you are a part.

Now you must move to a world community. This is not based upon ideology. This is not based upon theory or social science. This is based upon necessity, for the world's resources are diminishing, and the world's climate is changing.

Humanity will be facing a reality that as a whole it has never had to face before: ever-growing numbers of people drinking from a slowly shrinking well. World food production will be damaged and diminished by the changing climate and by the diminishing essential resources. It will produce upheavals and revolutions and convulsions unlike anything seen before. This will require greater cooperation and greater integration and greater assistance between nations, for you cannot have the nation next door collapse without putting your nation in peril.

It will be a humanitarian crisis on a scale never seen before, with millions of people having to leave their regions, unable to grow food or because of conflict and war. It is another great transition. It will be very difficult, and it must be guided by a greater wisdom and vision, or its outcome can be unfortunate indeed.

The Creator of all life is sending a New Message into the world to alert and to prepare humanity for the great change that is upon the world. It is this vision that must be clarified, for people cannot see and often will not see, their minds overwhelmed by the needs of the day and by their own fears and preferences and denial.

The leaders of the nations will try to maintain life as it has been, but the world has changed. You have now entered into a new world—a world of changing environments, changing weather and climate, changing circumstances, changing needs and changing priorities.

Seen from a greater perspective, this is the evolutionary transition from civilization to a world community. If humanity is to be free and to function without foreign intervention in the universe, it must have this greater unity, and this unity must be based not upon oppression but upon a greater development of the human spirit and capability.

The direction is clear. The goal is unavoidable. But what kind of world community will this be? Will it be a new foundation for human freedom and creativity? Will it be a cooperative society on a scale never seen before? Or will it be a cruel and oppressive regime, more cruel and oppressive than anything the world as a whole has ever faced?

The outcome will be determined by the thousands of decisions made by leaders and citizens as to how they will proceed through the Great Waves of change—whether they will choose cooperation or competition, whether they will realize that they must unite to survive, or will they fight and struggle for the last resources of the world as nations hoard, and as international trade begins to break down?

It is a situation unprecedented. You cannot base your understanding upon the past, the conditioning and circumstances of the past, for you are entering a new panorama now—new territory, unexplored regions.

Even the important solutions that have been brought to bear to serve the needs of people in the past will now be challenged by the immense scale of the human need. It is not merely a small population that needs support. It could be a hundred million people, and who has ever dealt with anything like that before?

Everything will become more expensive. Fuel will become more expensive. You cannot ship things around the world without great expense.

It will be a situation that will be not governed only by political will and political ideas, but by nature itself. For nature has been changed and damaged in this world, and it will set the terms of engagement for the future.

This is a harsh reality that few people, even amongst the experts in all fields, have really considered. It will not be a world based upon growth and expansion, but a world emphasizing stability and security for its peoples.

The kind of one-world community you will create will be determined by how you proceed, how you think and what informs your decisions. Whether you be the leader of the most powerful nation or the average citizen, this will be the case.

The shock of this will be so immense there will be great denial. There will be great disputation. There will be great controversy. And God's New Message will be denied, and even reviled, because it is telling people what they do not want to hear. They do not want to think that God has spoken again, and now they must reconsider their religious and political opinions, and even the consensus of opinion.

But the world will inconvenience you so much in this age of uncertainty that you will have to turn to a Greater Power. God knows this, of course. That is why there is a New Message from God in the world today—a Message unlike any message that has been sent into the world before; a Message that is vast, speaking on many subjects clearly, definitively; a Message for a literate world where people from all nations can hear at once through the advances of technology.

It is not a Message communicated in pastoral terms or in anecdotes or stories. For God is speaking to a literate world now, a literate world whose needs are tremendous and whose time to prepare is very short.

You cannot avoid your destiny. You cannot avoid the evolution of the world. To do so is to put yourself in jeopardy as an individual and to forfeit your promise for the future.

It will take courage, certainly. It will take determination and some self-discipline to consider what is being revealed here. But every day the world is giving testimony to this, and this will increase with time.

God knows what is coming, but humanity is blind and foolish. The world has changed, but humanity has not changed with it. The conditions of the world are shifting, but humanity insists that life be as it was before.

This will be convulsive for people, and many will perish. Many will collapse, not only in the poorer nations but elsewhere because they cannot see beyond what they have invested in before. They will lose what they have gained. And many will lose their life itself.

It is to mitigate this, so that the transition can happen with the least loss and disaster, that the New Message is here now—speaking of what people do not see, pointing to a future that people cannot or will not look into, going beyond the evaluations for the year to see what is really coming over the horizon.

You cannot avoid now the Great Waves of change. They are in motion and have been in motion for a very long time. It is like a tidal wave. It appears small on the horizon, but it has been traveling for a long ways. It has tremendous power behind it, enough to alter the coastline of a nation and to alter the destiny of many people.

Hear these words with an open mind. Set aside your ideas and your opinions. Let your mind be still so that you can hear and see. This is not a matter of debate for the intellect, for the Revelation exists beyond the realm and the reach of the intellect. You must listen and be patient, look and see.

The world is moving. Move with it, and your life will be secured. And you will be able to navigate the difficult times ahead. Resist it, avoid it, deny it, and you will face great tragedy.

That is why there is a New Message from God in the world and why it must come from God to have the power, the clarity, the vision and the wisdom to speak not only to what people think and believe today, but to speak of things that people are unaware of, to answer questions that have not even yet been asked, to anticipate the needs of the future—to know that future, to reveal that future.

If people really knew what was coming over the horizon, they would behave very differently. They would rethink their position. They would reconsider their ideas. And over time, if they responded wisely, they would see that they would have to stop complaining about everything and begin to take greater responsibility for their lives and circumstances. This is a very maturing process for the individual, and for the nations as well.

Feeding people will be a very, very great problem in the future. And preventing war and calamity, a kind of war that has rarely been seen in the modern era, will be a very great priority.

You will see this as nations erupt, as economies become stricken, as revolutions emerge, as the problem of feeding people and maintaining stability becomes ever more pressing and difficult to address.

Even the wealthy nations will be stricken, with many people unemployed, government leaders seeming impotent in the face of these changes, still trying to maintain what has occurred before and either unwilling or too afraid to express their views of what must really be done to address the situation.

The New Message speaks to the individual and what informs the individual, whether it be the power and the presence of Knowledge that God has placed within you to guide you, to protect you and to lead you to a greater life; or whether it be fear and social conditioning, the will of your family, your religion or your culture. What informs the decisions of individuals will make all the difference in the decisions that they make and the outcomes that are produced.

Whether this one-world community will be hellish or far greater and more beneficial than anything that has been created will be determined by the multitudes of decisions and what informs these decisions.

That is why the New Message speaks to the power and the presence of Knowledge in the individual, for here there can be no mistake. Here there can be no conflict. For God has put the same Knowledge in every person to guide their lives individually, but also to enable them to unite and cooperate with others.

As people fight against the Great Waves in denial, as they become more involved in their pursuits and distractions, and as nations and leaders become more unstable and dysfunctional, you will begin to see the need to turn to this greatest resource, the great endowment of the Creator that has been given to you.

For you must look to your life and to your family and to those whom you must care for. The welfare of the government may not be there in the future. You will have to become resourceful and compassionate. You will have to become stronger than you are today—mentally stronger, physically stronger, more determined, less pathetic, less complaining. The world will redeem you by requiring these things of you as an individual.

As individuals arise in your communities and societies with this strength, it will give greater promise that a beneficial outcome can and will be created.

The seas will rise. The crops will fail. Energy resources will become expensive, and there will be much conflict over who has them and who has access to them. Growing and distributing food will be a great difficulty, and there will be great civil unrest. Nations will not have the resources to solve their problems, so overwhelming will they be, happening at so many different fronts, all at the same time, like great waves crashing all at once, repeatedly.

God has given you the wisdom to prepare—to live in this world, to navigate this world and to be a source of contribution, a beneficial force in this world. But you must come to Knowledge, and take the Steps to Knowledge, to find the source of your strength, your power and your greater abilities. This will transcend your beliefs, your ideas, your notions and your assumptions about life, which are all based upon the past, and your theories, which are all based upon the past. The more fixed you are in your beliefs, the more difficult it will be for you to see, to know and to act with greater spontaneity and more appropriately to the real situations at hand.

For many people, the idea of a one-world community is terrifying. They think they will lose all privileges. They think they will be oppressed. They think it would be terrible in all respects. This is a possibility, that such a community could be like this. It is a real possibility. But you are going towards this, willing or not, ready or not, regardless of your perspective and point of view. This is your destiny. Just like it is your destiny to grow older in life and go through the stages of ageing and maturity.

Human civilization right now is very adolescent. It is not mature. It is wildly destructive. It is unaccountable to the future. It is pillaging the world as if you did not have a future. It is only beginning to work cooperatively, to sustain the flow of resources and to assure greater stability for nations that are unstable, that are facing great difficulty.

You will become a one-world community of some kind. What kind? Well, that will be determined by your decisions and the decisions of so many others. Do not neglect your own responsibility in this regard, for everyone's decisions will make a real difference.

This will be the most difficult task because you do not have much time. You do not have centuries to gradually transition into a different kind of civilization. You have years and decades only.

Nature will force this upon you. Your circumstances will force this upon you. You will have to adapt to a new world. And this adaptation will require, if you are to take care of the peoples of the world, a greater cohesion, a greater cooperation.

Nations can still be nations, and cultures can still be cultures. But the level of cooperation would have to be so much greater, or the world will descend into chaos. War will emerge in many places at once.

And there will be nothing the wealthy nations can do, for they too will be facing deprivation and restrictions.

It is to avoid this that the Calling is going forth, the vision is being given, the difficult reality is being presented that must be faced and considered. You have the strength to do this because you were designed to do this. You were designed to live at the time of the great transition.

This is the time of the great transition. Humanity's motivation will be increased by the reality that forces are intervening from the universe, seeking to take advantage of humanity's weakness and conflicts to establish themselves as the new leaders of this world. They come not with military power but with cunning and deception, for they are more advanced. They realize that war would destroy the resources of the world and the wealth of the world. They will use cunning and power in the mental environment to influence a weak and unsuspecting humanity.

Their presence is already in the world and has been here for decades. They too will prompt greater human unity if enough people can respond to their presence appropriately and recognize this as a real Intervention.

Facing the Greater Community is part of your maturing as a race. It is part of your evolution. It was always destined to happen, for humanity has built an infrastructure that other races can use. And humanity is destroying the wealth of the world, which has prompted Intervention.

You must begin to think in these larger panoramas now if you are to have any real clue as to what is occurring in the world and why things are happening at the pace that they are happening. Larger forces are at work now. You must begin to consider these, for they will change the circumstances and the opportunities of your life. And you avoid them or deny them at your own peril.

Despite the darkening skies and the Great Darkness that is in the world now, the Creator of all life is giving humanity its one great chance to unite to secure human sovereignty in this world and human freedom in this world in a universe where freedom is rare. It is an opportunity of unparalleled importance, but can only be considered by those who can face this human destiny and the Great Waves of change that are now upon the world.

The Great Waves will grow in time and become more exasperating, more damaging and more effective in altering the course of human affairs. You are just at the beginning of a great transition, a transition from separate, conflicting nations to a one-world community that must sustain and support itself and take care of the world's peoples.

It will be the beginning of a new kind of society, and if the decisions made are wise, if people can respond appropriately, then this will give great promise to the future, the freedom and the security of the human family.

For the universe around you is filled with powerful nations that are not free. And to be free in this larger environment, you must be united, self-sufficient and very discreet. It is an entirely different picture than what most people conceive of today regarding the possibility of contact with life in the universe.

As is the case with so many other things, many things will have to be reconsidered now in light of the great Revelation, in light of the great transition, in light of where you are all going—willing or not, ready or not, prepared or not.

God has given you the eyes to see and the ears to hear, but you must clear your mind. You must set aside your grievances, your complaints, your constant whining, your judgments, your unforgiveness in order to have this vision and to be able to hear and know.

It is not a matter of perspective. It is not a matter of being positive or negative. It is not a matter of whatever social or political theory you subscribe to. It is whether you can see and hear. It is fundamental, beyond the realm of the intellect.

And life is fundamental. Whether humanity can survive the great transition, and whether the outcome will be desirable or not, the transition is occurring and will occur. You cannot stop it, but you can add to it beneficially. You can be a source of inspiration and strength for those around you who are weak and vulnerable.

It will be a time that will require immense giving and contribution, not only from a few inspired individuals and dedicated organizations, but from peoples everywhere.

You will have to take care of the world and preserve its resources. In the future, humane methods will be needed to control and to diminish human populations. Consumption will have to be controlled. Individual freedoms, many of them, will be lost because you do not have the resources or the opportunities that you had before.

For many people, this will be frightening, and they will deny it. But this is where you are going. Prepare, and you will be able to navigate the difficult times ahead. In denial, you will be vulnerable, and the waves will overtake you. You will not see them coming. You will not anticipate them. And you will not be prepared for them.

The greatest security you have is the Knowledge that God has placed within you. You cannot stockpile for the rest of your life. You cannot run away and live underground somewhere. That will not work. Your greatest security is the quality of your relationships, the skills that you possess and your connection to Knowledge. These three things.

This is what you must build now. This is what you must cultivate now. Not only for the immediate future, but for the real future of your life and for the future of humanity.

CHAPTER 12

THE SHOCK OF THE FUTURE

As revealed to
Marshall Vian Summers
on April 30, 2011
in Boulder, Colorado

God seeks to prepare humanity for a new world, a new reality, and for its encounter with life in the universe, an encounter that will change and determine the future and destiny of humanity.

You are entering a new world—a world of environmental change, a world of violent weather, a world that is unpredictable, a world that will be unbalanced, with great political and economic difficulties. Nations will be shaken by revolution, and national economies will fail.

It is the outcome of many forces at work that have been at work for some time. The wise can foresee this. For everyone else, it will be a great shock—the shock of the future.

Do not look upon this as a great tragedy or something to avoid, neglect or deny, for this has your name upon it. You were sent into the world to serve the world under these conditions.

Though you perhaps have not been mindful of the Great Waves of change that are beginning to sweep across the world, they are moving nonetheless. It is not a time for complacency. It is not a time to project your ideas or beliefs. It is not a time to argue and debate endlessly.

It is a time to look and to see and to keep looking and watching, discerning the horizon, discerning the changing circumstances of life around you, discerning the change that is occurring in people's lives— unanticipated change, overwhelming change, beyond the normal parameters of life.

Perhaps your life has been changing internally and externally as if in preparation for something great that you would have to serve and be a part of. If this is your experience, then you can be certain that you are preparing for the new world, however unconsciously.

God has given you Knowledge to guide you and to prepare you, but Knowledge functions beneath the surface of the mind where people live. It is a greater Intelligence. It is discerning the movement of the world, and it is responding to the Creator.

God's New Revelation will speak to this part of you more than to your intellect, for this is the part of you that has never left God. Therefore, it is the part of you that can truly respond. It is the part of you that is wise and unconflicted. It is not afraid of the world, for it cannot be destroyed.

At the surface of your mind, you suffer over every little thing, and you have great anxieties about your future and well-being—always the fear of future loss, always the fear of the innumerable things that can happen to you and to those that you care for.

How can you ever know anything at this level, so filled with fear and ambition, so easily distracted, so easily manipulated, so easily controlled, so easily dominated by the opinions or the determinations of others?

The shock of the future will be a shock because you are unprepared. You have not been paying attention. You have been obsessed with other things of little or no significance. You have been caught up in the affairs of the day and in your own feelings and memories and regrets, not mindful of the world around you.

With preparation, there is no shock. There is only confirmation. Even that which is shocking will not overwhelm you. It will surprise and dismay you perhaps in the moment, but you will not be overtaken by it. You will not be paralyzed by it, frozen in fear without any idea of what to do.

When the ship begins to list and take on water, you will be ready. You will not be frozen. You will not go down with the ship.

God has given you the power to save you, not only from calamities in the world, but from every disaster and every miscalculation that you can make and experience along the way. You may pray to God for many things—for protection, for advantages, for a happy outcome— but God has given you the greatest possible gift. But if it is unknown or resisted or neglected, what else can God do for you?

God is not managing the affairs of the day. God is not moving the blood through your veins. God is not whipping up the winds or setting the temperature. This is a world of cascading events. It has no seeming order to it.

The forces of the world—the geologic and biological forces—were set in motion at the beginning of time. They are moving on their own. The degree to which humanity has upset the Earth's delicate balance will produce great events and is producing great events even at this moment.

But who is paying attention? Who is realizing the cause and the effect? Who is listening to the power and the presence that resides within them?

People vacillate between excitement and dread. They seek love as a kind of escape and intoxication to free them from the constant burden and overshadowing of fear and regret, whereas real love remains a mystery to them, real love emanating from Knowledge.

The world, in its great change, can serve you if you can approach it correctly. The shock of the world can prepare you. It can shake you out of your dreams of happiness and disaster. It can bring you to your senses. It can call upon your strengths and your determination and most certainly your compassion for people.

You are entering the age of human responsibility and cooperation. You must be a part of this, or your life will be wasted. Your life will be always threatened.

People want to retire into kind of a listless happiness, without a care, but when you see this, it is pathetic. It is sad. There is no intelligence. There is no inspiration. There is no honesty. There is no true connection with others. There is no service and contribution. They have cast themselves out of the meaning of life in their life of constant repose.

This is not for you. You did not make the long journey into this world and go through the stages of growth and development as a person with all of its difficulties simply to be put out on the pasture somewhere.

Those who sent you into the world are counting on your development and preparation. They know that that will be the source of meaning, happiness and contentment in your life.

Affluence will fade in the world. It will be lost by many people. The human need will become so great that it will call upon people everywhere to serve and to participate.

The ship is already taking on water, you see. It is already beginning to list to one side. Those who know this are being called to respond, to prepare themselves and to see where their contribution can be of the greatest benefit.

The future shock is for them right now—the shock of realization, the shock of having to turn your life in a new direction, the shock of realizing how little meaning and purpose have been in your life previously and how you have wasted yourself, your time and your valuable energy on things that had little or no promise.

This is the shock of the future, the future shock, happening at this moment as you begin to pay attention and to respond to the signs of the world.

God is calling you through these signs. God is not calling you to return to your heavenly state, but to enter into the world for the purpose that you have come.

This will change your values and your priorities. This will change what you look for in others. This will change what you value in yourself. This will change your relationship with time. This will change your experience of relationships. This will change your relationship with your mind and your body. This will change your relationship with everything. That is the shock.

Once you have turned this corner, if you can turn this corner, then you will be able to face almost anything. Though you may experience shock and dismay in the moment, it will not overtake you. Knowledge will become your foundation, and it is not shocked by the world. It is not even of the world. It is here to serve the world.

At the surface of your mind, you will continue to suffer over things, but they will be things of greater importance and significance, greater meaning and consequence, instead of little things that have no future and no destiny.

Your love will become authentic rather than delusional. It will be aimed at people who can really participate with you rather than those with whom you have no future and destiny.

God is calling you to respond, both within yourself and to the signs of the world. To see the signs, you must be looking and paying attention, not just here and there, but continuously. Like the birds in the air and the animals in the field, you are watching your environment. Just like them, you have a great need to do this.

Everything you value—your future, the people you care about, even your own life—will depend upon this. It is not looking with fear. It is not living in a state of trepidation. It is looking with clear eyes, with the power and the presence of Knowledge. That will make all the difference in whether you can see or not and whether you will look upon the world with dread and anxiety or with certainty, compassion and determination.

Your first commitment and engagement is to Knowledge because that is your commitment and engagement with God. If your engagement is authentic and not filled with your own ambitions and ideas, then you will have a foundation that will enable you to be a source of strength, purpose and reassurance for others. The need for reassurance at this moment is tremendous and is growing with each passing day.

Let the foolish be foolish. Let the ignorant be ignorant. Let the self-deceived be self-deceived. Let those who are lost in their opinions be lost in their opinions. Look for those who can respond. Look for those who can get off the [sinking] ship. Look for your true allies. For you will need strong companions now. You cannot be circumscribed by the weak minded and those who are too afraid to proceed.

This will change everything for you, as it must change, as it needs to change. It is the blessing of change. It is the difficulty of change. It is what will make you strong and powerful.

Do not think it will be easy, for it will not be easy. Do not think it will happen right away because it is a process of many stages and steps. Do not think that you are there already, for you do not know what you will have to face.

The shock of the future is with you now. The wise see before events occur and prepare accordingly. They do not wait to be overtaken in the last moment. They see the signs of the world. They determine the change in the weather, in the atmosphere, in the movement of things and in the response of not only people, but of the creatures of nature. They are watching.

They are not lost in their hobbies or their romances or their obsessions, only to be overwhelmed in the last moment. They do not follow the consensus belief. They do not follow what they are told by the leaders of government or religion. They do not follow the general opinions because people are blind and are not paying attention. They are not afraid to face challenge and difficulty, and so they do not pacify themselves with false assumptions. They do not take their cues from the weak and the fearful.

The gift of God is for everyone. The power of Knowledge is for everyone. But who can respond? The gifts of Heaven are for everyone, even living in a difficult and calamitous world. But who can receive them? Who can change their life and perspective to be in a position to experience this?

Even here the shock of the future is a gift—a gift of redemption. Awaking from one's own fearful Separation is a tremendous event. It calls the Powers of Heaven to you who are beginning to awake.

Let Knowledge be your guide, and let the world tell you where it is going and what is emerging on the horizon. Be watchful. Still your mind. Set aside your desires and your constant fear by taking the Steps to Knowledge. Receive the Revelation, the New Message for humanity.

You are blessed to even know of this. You are blessed to hear Our Voice. You are blessed to be shocked. You are blessed even to be disappointed, for this disappointment can free you from the past. You are blessed to be freed. You are blessed when people leave you. You are blessed when things fall away. For this begins to set the stage for a new life and a greater commitment and relationship with the Divine and with yourself and with others.

This is the world you have come to serve, and nothing but this service will render real meaning and true relationships for you. Understand this, and you will find the secret and the key to greater happiness, a greater meaning and a greater purpose, which are waiting to be discovered.

CHAPTER 13

BEING CENTERED IN A CRASHING WORLD

As revealed to
Marshall Vian Summers
on November 22, 2015
in Boulder, Colorado

To be intelligent means you are living in the moment and preparing for the future—the two fundamental aspects that require intelligence. You cannot do one without the other, for if you do not know how to be in the moment, you will not understand the signs of the world. If you do not prepare for the future, the world will overtake you, and you will be helpless and hopeless in its wake.

The great storms of the world are coming, the Great Waves of change, the great upheaval. For humanity has sown the seeds of this for a very long time. You are standing at the cusp of a new world experience. It is not the end of the world, but a great transition to a different kind of world reality.

Indeed, you have been sent into the world for this purpose—to participate in the world under these very circumstances that you may seek to avoid or to deny. It is because you do not know yourself. You are not yet connected to the deeper Knowledge that God has put within you—to prepare you, to guide you, to lead you to a greater life of service and meaning in a radically changing world.

The concern of Heaven is not merely that you will be fulfilled in the moment or what you may have for today, but that you may be prepared for the future in such a way that your greater gifts may come forth, and that the true purpose that has brought you here may be recognized, followed and correctly fulfilled.

You think for today and tomorrow only perhaps, or you are looking behind yourself with concern and regret. Without this deeper Knowledge in your awareness, you cannot yet prepare for what is to come. And you do not understand your past. In fact, you really do not understand anything very well.

Therefore, God must prepare you by giving you the steps to take to find this deeper strength and power that represents the immortal part of yourself that is not corrupted by the world, that is not terrified by the world, that is not even influenced by the world. It is the source of your strength, your courage and your integrity. It is also the source of your love, your compassion and your forgiveness.

While your mind struggles to understand, the deeper part of you already knows. It knows enough for you to take the next step that has been waiting for you.

For you must be centered in a crashing world. You must be strong. You must be purposeful. You must know where to give yourself and where to hold yourself back. You must be certain about who to be with and who not to be with despite any other possible attraction or intrigue that has gained control of your mind, which is running wild. It is chaotic, full of grievance and fear and fantasy. It is meant to be a servant to the deeper Knowledge within you, which represents your true Self. But it is out of control. It is harming you. It is leading you astray. It is pulled every which way by the world around you, and indeed it will be terrified by what is to come if Knowledge is not its guide and counsel.

Therefore, God is giving you what you really need for today and for tomorrow and for the remainder of your life on Earth. People look to the heavens wanting to have dispensations to try to fulfill their desires, ambitions and needs, but God is providing what is really essential.

For God knows why you are here, why you were sent and what it will require of you to face a changing world and the Great Waves of change.

You are living in Separation, but part of you has never separated from God. You are still connected. And God is going to redeem you through this Knowledge—not to take you out of the world, but to bring you here with greater purpose, meaning and relationship, things you cannot fulfill otherwise, try as you may.

Own everything you can, marry whoever is attractive, and you will still be lost. For you cannot find yourself without the power of Knowledge. You cannot be truly happy or satisfied with your life without the power of Knowledge.

God has already figured out your dilemma. It was figured out at the beginning of time. And it [Knowledge] lives with you today. It lives within everyone else. And it lives within all sentient beings and life in the whole universe. It is beyond the scriptures. It is beyond religious ideology and philosophy. It is the real power of Grace in your life.

It is with you here today, waiting for you to come to it in humility and sincerity—not to try to use it as a resource, for that is not possible; not to try to use it to gain love or wealth or security, for you cannot use Knowledge in this way. It is foolishness and arrogance to think that you can do these things.

But Knowledge is waiting for you to return, to come to it, seeking guidance and counsel, and over time allowing it to reshape your life, which it will do so naturally.

This is what it means to be truly centered, you see: that Knowledge is the center of your experience, the center of your life, the center of your Being, the center of your decisions, the center of your response to the world around you no matter what is going on.

Without this, you are lost in your thoughts, in your fears, in your preoccupations. You cannot see what is coming over the horizon, and you do not have the courage or the will to prepare. You are weak and vulnerable, easily persuaded by others, constantly adapting yourself to the expectations of others, seeking relationship perhaps, but unaware of who you are and where you really need to be going in life.

You cannot understand this with your intellect. It is vast. It is mysterious. It is profound. It is greater than anyone's understanding, but it is at the core of your true experience. It is what will save you. It is what will give you power. It is what will give you certainty and true direction and, in time, bring relationships of true value into your life.

For once you begin to take the Steps to Knowledge and continue to do so, you begin to end the Separation within yourself—the Separation from your worldly mind to the deeper Mind within you, that was you before you came into this world and will be you after you leave this world. While the soul wanders, Knowledge remains connected to its Source.

If you can understand what We are telling you here today, you will
see that it is the most important thing you could possibly consider. It
is the most important thing you could approach. For you have only
to look at the world around you to see the hopeless pursuits and
attempts at happiness and fulfillment.

The crisis of Separation continues within each person, no matter how
wealthy they are, no matter what they own or control. They may have
all the trappings of beauty, wealth and power. But they are unknown
to themselves and they are still lost.

God will not punish them for being lost because God has put
Knowledge within them. But they cannot return to their true state
until they begin to respond to what God has put within them and to
begin a preparation they did not invent for themselves—a
preparation both practical and mysterious. Practical in that it will
guide you in all practical matters, in all important decisions, in how
to understand yourself, others and the world with great clarity. But
mysterious because it cannot be controlled or understood by your
mind or the minds of others.

Once you come to the truth within yourself, you will realize you
cannot fulfill yourself. You cannot find real happiness and sustain it
here. You cannot protect yourself against a world becoming ever
more chaotic and uncertain with each passing day.

You must find your center in a crashing world. You needed it
yesterday. You needed it five years ago. You have always needed it.
And now you will need it ever more importantly, for things that you
depend upon or assume to be there for you may not be there for you.

Great tribulation is coming to the world, not because God wills it but because humanity has set it in motion. There is no punishment in God, but there is redemption there—for every person, religious or not, from every country, every tribe, every nation, every position in life. God has put Knowledge within them all, within you, waiting to be discovered.

The things that you think will keep you safe in the future will not keep you safe. You cannot rest your future upon weak assumptions that are easily changed by changing circumstances.

You have to be more intelligent than this. You have to be more resilient than this. You have to look ahead to see where you are going and to see what is coming your way. For God has given you the eyes to see and the ears to hear. But these are not the eyes that you see with or the ears that you hear with—not yet.

In the future, tens of thousands, even millions of people will be displaced by the rising seas and the world growing hotter and the crops failing everywhere. The disorder will be immense. And you will look at this with great fear and trepidation until you can find the strength of Knowledge, which is not afraid of what is coming, for it knows what is coming. Not precisely. Not the moment and the hour necessarily—not in all cases—but it knows what humanity has sown and what it will have to reap.

To Heaven, this is so very obvious, but you living on the surface of the Earth cannot see it yet. You do not yet have the eyes to see and the ears to hear. And so your vision is so limited. You are preoccupied with yourself, with your thoughts, with your plans, with your memories, with your problems, with your admonition against others. Your mind is taken up with these things.

Do not seek pleasantries alone. Do not try to pad your life with sweet and wonderful things. You must prepare for a world that will be much more dangerous and difficult to navigate. You may dismiss this at your own risk, but the world is giving you the signs with each passing day—the signs of great change that is underway and greater change to come.

God is going to save and protect you through the power of Knowledge. So you must seek this. You must take the Steps to Knowledge. You must build the bridge to Knowledge and redirect your life accordingly. For much of what you are trying to do at this moment is unnecessary for what you really need, both now and into the future.

You have to be centered. You learn, experience by experience, moment by moment. It will not come all at once, for you are not ready for that.

But if you take the Steps to Knowledge, it will grow stronger. You may question it, wanting things from it, but it will be silent because it is moving your life. It will speak when it needs to speak. In the meantime, you must follow and be as honest as you can about what you are doing and about your own thoughts and feelings.

God has given the preparation for you, to relieve your mind of its great burden of fear and condemnation, to relieve it of its great burden of preoccupation and foolish ideas that have no promise or value.

Living in Separation, you have tried to replace your experience of your Ancient Home with all kinds of things. Even if they seem perfectly all right, you cannot assure them for the future.

This is not a time to run away and hide and try to be safe somewhere, for there is nowhere to hide, really. Do not leave the city and live in the remote country because that will be even more dangerous.

But you are blessed to learn of the great preparation that God's New Revelation for the world is providing. For only God knows how to prepare you. You do not know how to prepare you. Only God knows what you will need to be prepared for. You do not know what you need to be prepared for. Here you do not become passive and detached from the world, trying not to feel anything because you will close the power of Knowledge within yourself if you do this.

You are meant here to participate, but to participate truly, you must be prepared. And you are not the source of the preparation. Be grateful it is so. It is a great blessing indeed.

Knowledge will teach you how to navigate the changing world. But first it must free you from the burden of your current conditions, mostly your mental and emotional conditions, which weigh upon you more heavily than almost anything else. You must free your mind so the power of your mind can be used purposefully.

Do not live only for the moment, for that is a fool's paradise. You must prepare for the future, or you will be a victim of the future. If you could really see what is coming, you would understand perfectly what We are telling you here today.

The world will get hotter. Great weather events will have ever more destructive power. Humanity has unleashed a great change upon the world through its misuse of the world—its greed, its corruption, its plundering of the world's resources with never a thought for tomorrow.

You are going to have to now live in this new world. Your children will have to live in this new world. Who will prepare them? Who will prepare you? Who will give you courage and strength and real determination?

Political leaders cannot do this. Economic theories cannot do this. As humanity struggles to cope and to survive, you will have to take greater steps—the Steps to Knowledge.

God is not going to come and save humanity in the eleventh hour, but God has given you the power of Knowledge to guide you and prevent you from giving your life away to meaningless and hopeless things. This is how God will save you, and through you others, and through others the whole world, in time, if enough people can respond.

Do not think you will be passive, sitting around waiting for messages, for you will be at work—working on your circumstances, correcting your behavior, setting things aside, taking things on, making important decisions and having to be responsible for the outcome of those decisions. There is no passivity here. You are not going to be led like a little child. For the world you are facing will be hazardous, and you must be very strong and very determined to deal with it.

You will see immense suffering around you, immense travail. People will act foolishly in the face of the Great Waves of change. They will elect dangerous officials. They will give themselves to dangerous pursuits. They will take sides against others. They will retreat into fear and defensiveness. You will see this everywhere, in all nations.

It will be very disturbing. It will be very difficult. It will be heart wrenching. But you must find your center and hold fast to this in the challenges to come. And from this center you will know what to practice and what not to practice. You will take a journey of many steps, for you are not ready for a greater life yet.

You will have to overcome certain tendencies within yourselves. And Knowledge will give you the power and clarity to do this. You will have to change your relationships with certain people who are holding you back or taking you away. Knowledge will give you the strength and certainty to do this.

You will have to build the foundation of your life, practically. It will be a lot of work, but it will be redeeming. It will be purposeful. And it will give you meaning in the moment and strength for the future.

This is not the end times, but it is the end of the world as you have known it. Do not subscribe to such ideas, for they were given in ancient times. They only have meaning symbolically. But many things will come to an end, and this will impact people greatly.

For this, most people are unprepared—circumstantially unprepared, emotionally unprepared, spiritually unprepared. And that is why God is giving the great preparation for the world in a New Revelation for the world.

For God gives people what they truly need, both now and for the future. Not what they want in the moment, which in so many cases would only weaken them further and make it more difficult for them to respond.

God is not going to do things for you. God is going to teach you how to do things for yourself and for others. God is not going to give you miracles. God is going to give you the steps to become powerful and certain and compassionate in a world of ever-growing discord.

God is not going to make your life work or cast a spell over you to make your past and your history disappear. God is going to teach you how to use your past and history to gain wisdom and strength, for surely it is a demonstration of what life is like without Knowledge, if seen correctly.

When you pray, pray that your relationship with Knowledge will become stronger. Pray that you will have strength and courage and compassion. For you need this today, and you will certainly need it in the future. When you pray for others, pray that Knowledge will become strong within them so that they may find the true pathway and course of their life.

God is giving you a whole new platform upon which to build a new and stronger life, a platform that can survive the Great Waves of change and gain meaning from it and provide service within it.

Right now you are like sleeping on the beach, and the great tsunami waves are coming. You are sleeping there, dreaming of what you want and what you are afraid of. While the animals seek higher ground and the birds fly away, the people are lying on the beach as if nothing is happening at all.

You must take this journey. Do not try to do it for other people. Do not try to have them do it with you. For each person must respond. For your children, teach them how to follow and listen to their own deeper experience and give them a demonstration of courage and integrity from yourself, from your own life.

You cannot save everyone. But you are not sent here to save everyone. You must build your foundation, your true foundation. From that, the true service that you are here to provide will naturally come forth. At this moment, you cannot determine what it will be, what it will look like, what it will mean. For you are not ready. You do not yet have the eyes to see.

You must get serious about your life. It is not a game. It is not a shopping spree. It is not a vendetta against other people. It is not a fantasy built upon fantasy. You are going to have to become strong enough to take care of yourself and others, without becoming a victim yourself.

You do not know how to achieve this, and your ideas most likely will do you more harm than good. That is why God has sent the preparation into the world—a warning, a preparation and a great blessing for a struggling humanity, facing now change on a scale never seen in the world before, given now to a humanity standing at the threshold of space, a Greater Community of life in the universe, with which it must learn to contend.

People live their lives as if nothing has really changed. But, in fact, everything has really changed. The climate of your world is changing. The resources of your world are being diminished. The world is being interfered with from races from beyond, who see the great opportunity to take control here without the use of force.

God is alerting you, preparing you, warning you, trying to awaken you from your troubled sleep, from your dreams and preoccupations, from your tendencies and habits so that you can find your real strengths, your real qualities, the real courage and value of your life, which is alive within you underneath everything that has been put on top.

God's first purpose is to unburden you, to relieve you of those things that are harming you and others, to relieve you of your crown of thorns—your aggravations, your contempt for others and yourself, your regrets, your ignorance. God's first purpose is to unburden you.

Before you can know what comes next, this unburdening must take place. And it will take time. It does not happen overnight. In this, you must learn to follow without knowing what it looks like around the other side of the mountain. You must live without definitions for your future. You must live without many of the conclusions that you rely upon today, which will be hopeless in the times to come.

Not everyone will be able to respond to this. Not everyone will find it in time. Many will reject it because of their religious beliefs or positions, unable to see that it really is a true Message and preparation from God.

You can do nothing for them. You must continue on yourself. The Calling is for you. They have their own calling, to which they may or may not respond. You must respond to yours.

You must be centered in a crashing world—courageous, purposeful, affected but not overtaken by things around you, impacted but not overwhelmed by what you see and hear.

Here you do not need to be so armored because your center is Knowledge. You have returned to yourself as you really are, not as the world has made you. And with this, the Power of Heaven can move through you, mysteriously. It is a perfect Plan. And it is come at just the right time.

CHAPTER 14

RESILIENCE

As revealed to
Marshall Vian Summers
on December 10, 2014
in Boulder, Colorado

Humanity is standing at the threshold of the greatest world change it has ever experienced, a world facing a changing climate, great disruption, great economic and social discord as humanity, unprepared as it is, faces a new world experience—a more difficult world, a world of shrinking resources and violent weather, a world where humanity will have to make very fundamental decisions as to how it will respond and prepare for a different kind of future.

People in the world are still asleep or oppressed. The wealthy are asleep, still dreaming their dreams of affluence and personal fulfillment while most of the world struggles to survive under the weight of poverty and political and religious oppression.

Into this seemingly hopeless situation, the Lord of the universes has brought a great Message for humanity, a New Revelation for the world—a great warning, a great empowerment and a great preparation.

If you could truly recognize the condition of the world and your own condition within it, you would see the great need for God to speak again. And God has spoken again, giving humanity now the largest Revelation ever brought to this world to prepare humanity for a new world and to prepare humanity for its engagement with a universe full of intelligent life—a Greater Community of life, a great panorama of life, a community of which humanity knows nothing at all, a non-human universe where freedom is rare.

If you have the honesty and the humility to begin to face the real condition of your life and of your world, you will recognize that the great Revelations of the past cannot prepare humanity for what it is facing now. Given in antiquity, they were appropriate for their time and their place and still hold great wisdom and great teachings for humanity, but they cannot prepare you for what you are facing now.

God knows this, of course, but humanity is still lost in its preoccupations, its admonitions, its conflicts, its religious strife and sense of supremacy.

It is time for you now to learn the true nature of human spirituality, your connection with your Source and how God works within the world, working through people from the inside out.

God knows that humanity is in a precarious situation, from which it cannot save itself. It is too blind. It is too preoccupied. It is too filled with contempt and conflict. It is not strong enough or united enough to prepare on its own. With honesty and humility, you will see these things, for they are undeniable.

You are facing a situation of great complexity. You will need a Revelation from God, as well as your own intelligence and resources, to contend with this, to prepare for this, to survive within this, and, if you can do these things, to build a greater future for the human family—a greater security for the world, a greater unity for the human family, a greater strength and a greater permanence in this world and within the Greater Community in which you have always lived.

The great Messengers of the past, who have all come from the Angelic Assembly—the Jesus, the Buddha and the Muhammad— stand with the Messenger who is now being sent into the world, the only Messenger sent with a great Revelation from God.

What a challenge this will be for everyone who can respond. What a challenge on top of the great challenge of the new world and of life in the universe.

But God has given you a greater strength and a greater purpose for being in the world at this time. Deep beneath the intellect, deep beneath your personal mind—which has been so conditioned, directed and manipulated by the world around you—this greater Intelligence has your strength and the power to navigate the great change that is coming. It has the clarity and the connection with God to resonate with God's New Revelation for the world.

People's ideologies will be challenged, for God brings great correction to humanity's understanding of the great traditions and of the meaning of spirituality, the purpose of humanity and its ultimate destiny.

What a great challenge this will be for people who have built their whole life on a set of beliefs and admonitions, when in fact they know really nothing at all about God's Greater Plan and Purpose here.

God has given you now the strength. It lives within you, deep beneath the surface of the mind. It is uncorrupted. It is unafraid. For it represents the eternal part of you that is still connected to God, you see. It is not threatened by the world. It is not living in a state of constant anxiety, as your personal mind is. It is not living in a world of obsession and distraction, anxiety and contempt—the very things that rule your personal mind and the minds of all who dwell here.

God understands these things. There is no judgment against humanity. There is no punishment awaiting you. But you must prepare for eventualities. You must gain the position to see what is coming over the horizon with clear eyes, without all your former beliefs and political persuasions to color your vision and to blind you.

It is not enough that a few prescient individuals are becoming aware of the great change, and even that understanding is incomplete, you see. For they cannot see the whole picture, for that must be given in Revelation.

If you are able to begin to face these things, which is a great challenge, We understand, you will feel weak; you will feel helpless. You may even feel hopeless. You will wonder how humanity can ever pull itself through this, how it will ever be able to unite and to pool its wisdom and intelligence, skills and technologies in a positive direction, rather than wasting them away in war and conflict. For there is no time for that now. There is no time for such foolishness.

You will wonder if there is any hope at all. You will look around you, and you will see the sleeping minds everywhere. You will look out into the world, and you will see corruption and conflict, struggle and strife, and terrible poverty everywhere. And you will wonder, "How can this ever work?"

Here your personal mind does not have an answer. Here what you have learned and been taught to think does not have an answer. Your answers, even if they were appropriate, are only partial, for you will need a thousand answers now, and you do not have them all.

It is your Creator who will intervene in the world, which only happens, perhaps, once in a millennium to alter the direction of humanity, to plant the seeds of greater wisdom, power, strength and cooperation here at the time of greatest opportunity and greatest need.

You will have to turn to this strength that God has put within you and within others. And you will have to take the steps to this greater Knowledge, for you cannot find the way on your own. You will have to recognize that you cannot rule your life like a tyrant. You cannot rule your life, really, at all, but you must manage your mind and affairs and know the source of your strength that lives within you, at this moment, waiting to be discovered.

It is being called forth now, for the skies are darkening, and the great change is coming—striking the shores, burning the deserts, drying up the croplands. It is here, it is there, growing in frequency and potency and destructiveness.

You cannot be pathetic. You cannot be weak. You cannot simply pray for miracles, for God has sent you here to do the real work that must be done—your unique purpose and activity, of which you are yet unaware. For it is very different from your goals and your fantasies about yourself.

If you could recognize your own need—being a stranger to yourself, living a life of struggle, living a life of mundanity, living a life of indignity and frustration—you will see your need for Revelation. It is this same honesty, whether you are looking without or looking within, that will bring you to this point of recognition.

Perhaps you feel you have achieved great things. Perhaps you have pride. Perhaps you look down upon others who have nothing or who fail in their attempts to have what you have. But you too are standing at the threshold of the great change and do not have an answer.

Everything you have acquired can be lost. Everything you believe can be shattered. Everything you assume to be true can be undone. For you know not yet the Power that has brought you here and what you are really here to accomplish.

God is now speaking to a literate world, not primitive tribes who live in warlike societies and know nothing of social development and personal freedom. God is now speaking to a world of global communication and growing global awareness.

So now the Revelation is not brought in pastoral themes or anecdotes, in stories that must be interpreted by experts or commentators. It is brought in the simplest language with much repetition and clarification. It is brought in this way so that it can be translated easily into other languages and expressed easily and understood easily for people of all social standings, of all social positions. The poorest person in the world can understand. And yet it is so deep, you cannot fathom it. Its simplicity expresses its great depth.

This is the miracle of your time, given at a time of the greatest need, a need so great that few people are even aware of it or can face it honestly. This is the miracle of your time. This is the miracle of your life. For you have been found like a speck upon the ocean, drifting aimlessly, hopelessly. Whether you live in poverty or splendor, it is all the same.

It is not enough that a few people in the world are able to regain their true and natural state. The calling must be now for greater numbers of people to step forward, for this ship is listing. It is taking on water. But people are still sleeping on the deck, luxuriating in the sunlight, unaware that the very vessel that they stand upon is imperiled.

Who will know these things? Who can look without condemnation? Who can look with compassion, even for those who err so grievously?

Humanity is living in a dream, a dream of Separation. Yet now it has created a condition for the world that will change the landscape of the world and everything upon it.

Now you have reached a point where races in the universe will seek to gain control of your world. So valuable it is, so rich it is. You know not of its wealth in a universe of barren planets and struggling societies.

God's Revelation will reveal what life is like in the universe, and what you must know to survive there and to build and preserve your freedom there, which will be a great challenge.

But first you must know your strength, and you must build your resilience to live in a changing world, to live in a new world. You must have a greater strength to overcome your doubt, your fear and your weakness, your preoccupations and your tendencies.

God has given this to you. It has been with you all along—waiting to be discovered, waiting for the time when it must be called forth, waiting for the circumstances around you, which will make it necessary and imperative for your well-being and for your fulfillment in the world.

For you have come here to give and to serve. You have unique gifts, which must be opened within you, for you cannot open this yourself.

The deeper Knowledge within you can reshape your life and prepare you for your new life in a new world. Perhaps you cannot yet see that this is the greatest possible gift that could be given to you.

Any prayers you make to your Source have already been answered because of what has been placed within you to guide you, to correct you, to give you strength and certainty and compassion in a world where people will be increasingly disorganized and disorderly, filled with anxiety and apprehension.

You must build the awareness and then the resilience. At this moment, you are so easily shaken, even shaken by your own feelings, your own doubts, your own nightmares.

Think how shaken you will be when you see the world unraveling around you, when you have to face the new world, when you have to face the reality that human freedom is being threatened by Intervention from beyond.

With this understanding, you will realize you must build your strength. And God has provided the Steps to Knowledge to build this strength and this capacity to understand and to know and to see; to learn how to view your own errors and weaknesses with compassion and learn how to manage them, control them and correct them if possible. You do not have this strength yet, not sufficiently.

You are governed by weakness. You must be governed by strength. Certainly, that within you which is weak must follow that within you which is strong. Certainly, that which is foolish within you must follow that which is wise.

What is strong and wise within you is the Knowledge God has placed within you, a Knowledge that represents your eternal state and connection to your Source.

Without this, you can only believe in God, fall down and worship out of fear that God will punish you should you fail. But this is not the strength you will need to regain your connection to your Source or to survive and navigate in the new world around you.

Cleverness, ingenuity, philosophy, technology—without Knowledge, these things will all fail you. They are not enough. And you do not know how to use them effectively because you are still guided by your personal mind, which is fearful and driven and arrogant.

The mind must serve Knowledge. Knowledge will always serve God. This is the true hierarchy within you. This is the true ascension of power.

Everything is important here. Your body is important as a vehicle of communication in the world. Your mind is important as a vehicle of communication in the world. Knowledge within you is in the world to communicate. For you have been sent from those beyond, who are watching you even now.

It is this awakening that must occur. It is the resilience that must be built. It is the strength, the compassion and the determination that must arise within you—not from your ideas, not from your willfulness alone, but from the greater strength that lives within you.

Only it has the power to lead you forth into a new world and into a Greater Community of life, which is your destiny, and within which you have always lived, and for which you must now prepare.

CHAPTER 15

THE VISION

As revealed to
Marshall Vian Summers
on January 27, 2013
in Boulder, Colorado

Humanity has the seeds of greatness, despite its errors, its ignorance and its corruption. For spirituality is still alive in this world, where it has died and been forgotten in so many others. The fire of love is still burning here, in the minds and hearts of many, many people—a fire that has grown cold in so many other worlds in the universe around you.

Humanity knows not of its greater promise and greater potential, for it struggles with the very forces that have destroyed the power of love and Knowledge in other worlds—the very forces of greed, expediency, corruption, conflict, war and deprivation.

Think not this is unique to this world and to the human family, for such things have been a part of every great nation's evolution in the universe around you. But many of those nations beyond your world have never known freedom, have never known compassion. Suppressed from the beginning, they have evolved technologically, but not in any other way that is meaningful at all.

Humanity knows not of its greater promise and its potential for the future. Yet the future that will give humanity stability, security and protection from collapse within the world and from intervention from without will be a very different looking world from what you see today, and very different from what the vast majority of people expect and are planning for at this moment. For if humanity's desires and ambitions were to be fulfilled in the future, civilization would collapse and be overtaken by other nations in the universe, who are already looking at the world with great determination.

The future world for humanity, should it be successful in making this great transition, is a world that few people can see today. Yet it represents growth and maturity in the universe, particularly amongst advanced worlds that have been able to maintain individual freedom, and to benefit from its gifts, and to minimize the effects of its chaotic expressions.

This is evolution. But evolution follows the decisions of the intelligent races of which it is a part. Should humanity continue in its desperate course, it will deplete the world's resources and so destabilize the world's climate that it will only be inhabitable by a very small percentage of the human population, and under greater duress for those who can survive. Think not this has not happened in the universe around you, for environmental collapse has happened countless times with grave and tragic consequences so often as the result.

The future world will have to be built from the ashes of the old world and from the desire, compassion and wisdom of those who can see and who recognize that humanity is turning a great corner and passing through a great threshold at this time.

For the future world that will be greater than your past will have to be approached through a very difficult and dangerous time of transition—a time where many things will fall away; a time where there will be great and increasing environmental, social and economic instability; a time when there will be a great risk of war and competition over who will gain access to the remaining resources.

Nations will become unstable. There will be violent revolutions, even within stable countries. There will be increasing rancor between nations, vying and contesting over the few remaining unspoiled parts of the world. The possibility for humanity to break down is very great under these circumstances and should never be underestimated. Do not be fooled by blind optimism, for you must face the realities of living in a world of shrinking resources and environmental instability.

Here humanity has a great choice, not to be made merely by the leaders of nations, but by citizens everywhere as to which path they will follow. Will they follow the path of contention, competition and war? Or will they seek to find ways to restore the world, to husband its resources and share it equitably so that humanity can have a future, a future greater than its past? Here human unity and cooperation are not driven by a great ideal or by a religious philosophy, but by sheer necessity itself, for the alternatives are far too grave and tragic to even consider.

Do not complain about this or think it is a great misfortune for you, for you have been sent into the world at this time to be a part of this great transition. If you can discover the greater Knowledge that God has placed within you—that is there to guide you, protect you and lead you to a greater life of fulfillment and contribution—then you will be able to use these circumstances beneficially, to be part of a greater force for good in the world, a force that will be greatly needed and must be expressed through the intentions and the wisdom of individuals in many, many places.

You are at a great crossroads. Choose one path and it will determine your destiny. Choose another path and it will determine your destiny. Here you must have vision. You cannot simply act out of haste and expediency. You cannot simply act out of the desire for power and wealth in the moment, or you will forfeit the future and create an outcome more terrible than you can even imagine.

Here God is not punishing humanity. It is not God's wrath, for God has no wrath. That is a human invention—an angry God for angry people. But God is allowing humanity to determine its fate in this world, and to choose its course of action, and to determine individually and collectively which way it will go, facing this great divide in the road.

If humanity chooses the path of contention, competition and war, then you can follow this in your imagination to see how dreadful and dire the circumstances would be. In fact, it is more dire than even you can imagine.

To choose the alternative is to choose to live differently, using much less of the world's resources and thinking of yourself not merely as part of a group, a tribe or a nation alone, but as a world citizen now working to preserve the stability of the world and the continuance of human civilization, which has been built over a very long period of time and has advanced and progressed because of the noble work of countless people who have given their lives to build certain aspects of this civilization. Though this civilization is highly imperfect and filled with error and corruption, it still has magnificent potential.

If you could venture around the universe, your local region of space, you would see how great this potential is in contrast to most other nations. You would be shocked and dismayed at the lack of freedom in these realms. You would look at the life in these worlds and realize it would be utterly oppressive for you. Many have been greatly diminished through war and conflict, within themselves and between themselves and other nations in the universe. The lessons here are profound, grave and very necessary to recognize.

Take the easy path, the path of living for the moment, having everything you want, and you will be the engine of war in this life. You will follow the path that so many other worlds have followed to an inevitable outcome of deprivation and chaos.

But God has sent a New Message into the world to warn of the outcome here and to give humanity a greater promise, for humanity has this greater promise. Despite its tragic history and its endless conflicts, it still has this greater promise. And you as an individual have this greater promise because God has put Knowledge within you to guide you, Knowledge you have not yet discovered, but which you need desperately in all of your endeavors.

The vision is a sustainable world. That means that the Earth will provide you everything you need, for you cannot go out in the universe to seek resources you have destroyed here on Earth, or you will fall under the persuasion of foreign powers. They will even encourage you to do this, for that is how dominance could be gained in this world by those who watch you from afar.

No, humanity will have to be self-sufficient. It will have to be united sufficiently. And it will have to be very discreet.

For free worlds do not coexist easily with worlds that are not free. Here you must be very careful. This will change your ideas of space travel and visiting other worlds, as if it were some kind of spiritual quest or some kind of fascinating tourism. Dispense with these notions, for they are absurd and unnatural in the universe.

Humanity will have to become very responsible and very careful in what it projects out into space, how it governs its world and shares its resources and so forth.

From this point in time, you may say, "Well, I can't even imagine such a world. I don't think it is possible." But it is not only possible. It is necessary. For the alternative is too terrible to consider.

Therefore, you must listen and be open to a new reality and to your participation in building this reality, for it will not come in and of itself. If determined individuals are not oriented towards it, then humanity will take its otherwise course of action. It will fall into disarray.

Therefore, you must have a great heart, great strength, a great purpose and a great vision, which Knowledge within you will give you once you are ready to receive. You need this because you need to emerge out of your pathetic life, your pathetic endeavors, your tragic ideas and involvements. Considering who you are and what you are really sent here to do, your life currently is pathetic and unfortunate and misguided.

Accept this, for it speaks of your greatness. But to adopt your greatness, you must face your weakness as objectively as you can. And you must hold a vision for humanity that seems impractical, unrealistic, maybe even impossible, but necessary nonetheless. For it is a Vision of Heaven. It is the Will of Heaven. But the Will of Heaven must express itself through the minds, hearts and actions of people everywhere.

Your future will be very different. It will have a much smaller human population. Vast parts of the world will have to be left in their natural state to begin to rebuild the climates of the world. Trade will be much more local than it is today, for the resources to bring things from all over the world will not be there sufficiently, except in very rare situations. The rivers will have to be cleansed. The lakes will have to be cleansed. The skies will have to be cleansed.

You will have to guard your borders to space very carefully and be very cautious about any other races visiting here. Your few allies in your local region of space will not seek to gain relations with you until you have reached a stable and settled state in this new world, for they realize that their presence here would create doubt and confusion, for you do not yet have the skill to tell friend from foe in this regard.

Humanity will have to earn its freedom. It will have to earn its insulation in the universe. It will have to outgrow its adolescence and its childish fantasies about its self-importance in the universe, and what the universe really is, and what is occurring out there.

To make this possible, the Creator of all life has sent, as part of the New Message for humanity, a teaching on the reality and spirituality of life in the universe to give you a true account of what is occurring beyond your borders and a sober understanding of what you must do here on Earth to prepare to be in this Greater Community as a free and self-determined race.

Your future world will be a world of changing climate and limited food production. The deserts will grow. The oceans will rise. Therefore, the lands that can produce food must be very carefully cultivated and protected. War and contention between nations will be limited out of necessity. As much self-sufficiency as possible will have to be established wherever humanity can maintain its position and its infrastructure.

There will have to be great compliance, and, to a certain extent, individual freedom will be limited. For in this world, you cannot do anything or have anything or be anything you want. But that is okay because you did not come into the world to indulge yourself in this way. You have been sent into the world to serve the world and to contribute to the furtherance and the building and the refinement of human civilization.

That is your true purpose. And if you could find your deeper nature and begin to respond to it, you would see indeed this is true for you regardless of your personality, your habits, your beliefs, your religion or your nationality.

If enough people can come to realize the power of Knowledge within them, the deeper Mind that God has placed within them, then such a world can be created and achieved with a minimum of stress and destruction.

Indeed, your great adversary in the future will be nature itself. You will have to find ways to protect yourself from the increasing instability of the natural world that is the product of human abuse, corruption and pollution. It will be a struggle with nature more than a struggle with one another.

Nature here is a powerful adversary and must be understood and respected above all things. But at present, humanity has lost its contact with nature. It thinks it can turn the world into anything it wants. It thinks it can turn the deserts into farmland. It thinks it can turn its cities into playgrounds. It thinks it can harness all the powers of the Earth for its own indulgences, desires and intentions. But it is a fool's paradise, and everyone in the Greater Community who has passed through these developmental stages understands the meaning of this.

Human freedom and freedom in the universe is not a right. It is a privilege. It is a reward built by the tireless efforts of generations of individuals making it possible for freedom to exist and to be maintained and to reap the benefits of its great creativity and productivity while minimizing the difficulties and chaos that it can produce between peoples at times, if it is not guided by Knowledge.

Your future world will have a much smaller population, but this must be orchestrated and not be the product of the destruction of the human family. But the transition between the world you have today, which is crumbling, and the future world that is your greater promise is a great gulf.

It is as if you were standing at the edge of a great chasm and you were looking across the chasm to the other side, wondering how you were going to get there. There is no magic lift that is going to lift you over this chasm. There is no bridge that is going to appear magically to take you there. You are going to have to climb down into this chasm, go through it and find the way up the other side.

There is a way, and God is showing the way in the New Revelation. For the old Revelations of God cannot provide for this, for that is not their purpose. They were not designed for this. But now humanity has reached a great threshold, perhaps the greatest it has ever encountered—the destabilization of the world and its encounter with a universe of intelligent life, a non-human universe where freedom is rare.

You must understand these things if you are to ever discover your greater purpose for being in the world. You must understand these things if you are to understand your deeper nature and why you are in conflict with yourself over what you want and what you need. You must understand these things to realize that there is a voice of wisdom within you, and there are many voices of weakness within you. You must be able to hold that which is true, even if it seems improbable or even impossible, given the world today. You must have the Vision of Heaven. It must be in your heart, not just in your mind.

Think of this future world. It will not be an easy world. It will not be a paradise. It will not be a world where you will have everything you want, endlessly. It will be a world of great responsibility and cooperation. It will be a world where you will have to take care of other people and be a true participant in your nation and culture. It is a world where human corruption will be limited even if it cannot be eradicated. It will be limited out of necessity, for humanity cannot afford war or revolution in a world like this.

Your position in the world will be more fragile than it has been in the past, and you will be threatened by forces in the universe who will seek to gain dominion here without the use of force, using the powers of persuasion and inducement or discouragement. You will be battling an unstable climate and the reduction of resources. Everything will have to be utilized well and carefully.

But it will be a world of great spiritual power and great security, greater than any time in human history, if such a world can be achieved. It will be a world where human ingenuity will be highly valued. And the power of Knowledge will be available to many more people than is the case today.

You must hear what I am saying to you. It is not the world you want. It is the world that will be and that must be created. And you want this, and you will want it increasingly as the world around you becomes ever more unstable, ever more challenging, ever more dangerous.

Here you must stop complaining about the world and use that energy that you spend in a meaningless way and wastefully complaining and criticizing others, to begin to build the Four Pillars of your life, the overall foundation for enduring a time of great change and upheaval. You must take the Steps to Knowledge to find the greater power that God has given you, which exists beyond the realm and the reach of the intellect. And you must look upon the world following the counsel and guidance of God's New Revelation, which alone has the power and clarity to produce a greater future for humanity.

Here all the religious teachings of the world will find their resonance, if they can be understood correctly. For they were given to build human civilization, world civilization, and they have been partially successful in doing this.

Now human civilization must be protected and must endure the Great Waves of change that are coming to the world and must be protected against intervention, persuasion and manipulation from forces from beyond the world, who are here to take advantage of human weakness, division and expectations.

Do not shrink from this, for this is your life. This is your future. This is the world you are going to hand to your children. This is the world you are going to have to deal with when you finally grow up and stop indulging yourself in your fantasies and wasting your time and your life through meaningless engagements with others.

It is a world that will require human maturity, human wisdom and human cooperation on a scale never seen before. In this, humanity can find its redemption, its power and fulfill its destiny in becoming a free and self-determined race in the universe.

This is the vision. You must hold this vision if you are to build such a future and not let the tragedies of the past and the consequences of the past and the ignorance of humanity, the stupidity of humanity, discourage you or rob you of this vision. Or you will lose your destiny here.

Here you must forgive your past. You must forgive others and see that it all represents the need for Knowledge within yourself. Your failures, their failures, the failures of the past, the likely failures of the future must all be seen clearly and objectively and recognized as a demonstration, a vast and compelling demonstration of the need for Knowledge.

That is why God has given you the Steps to Knowledge. For the first time in the history of this world, God has given the Steps to Knowledge for people everywhere, not just for saints and sages, or great artists or humanitarians. The prescription for success and the warning against failure are now being provided as never before.

Do not deceive yourself in thinking that this is a negative assessment of the future. It is simply being honest. And if you can be honest with yourself and objective in viewing the world, you will see these things. They are clear as day to those who can see.

People insist upon the world they want because they are afraid of the world. And they are so given to their desires and their beliefs and their preferences they cannot see clearly what is occurring around them, and even within them. So they mismanage their health. They mismanage their relationships. They mismanage the use of the world. They fall into contention with themselves, with others and with life itself.

Look with clear eyes, and you will see these things demonstrated all around you. But you must not look with condemnation if you are to have the strength and the energy and the focus to hold the greater vision that must be held by increasing numbers of people.

If God's New Revelation can be made available to them, they will be able to see. And they will be able to recognize that Knowledge is the most powerful force in the universe, and that it lives within them, waiting to be discovered.

Remember, humanity is facing a fundamental decision about which way it will go. And it will go the way it is going now unless enough people decide otherwise. Though they cannot create the new world right away, they must build the foundation for it to exist, which will require generations of people's efforts and dedicated action.

You may wonder: Will people actually do these kinds of things in spite of their self-interests? We say, if they are guided by Knowledge, they will do these things, for that is the greatness that lives within them.

Here you must have faith not only in the outcome, but you must have faith in the power and presence of Knowledge within you. If that is a distant unknown reality, then you must take the Steps to Knowledge to find the source of your strength, your integrity and your greater mission in being in the world at this time under these circumstances.

The blessings of Heaven go with you in this. Whatever religion you are a part of, whatever nation you live within, whatever your social standing, whatever your economic reality—the Calling is there, the power of Knowledge is there. It must come forth from the many now and not just the few. This is the Will of Heaven. May this become then the intention of humanity.

CHAPTER 16

THE FUTURE OF HUMANITY

As revealed to
Marshall Vian Summers
on May 12, 2010
in Boulder, Colorado

Humanity has a great future, but an uncertain future—a future that is now being challenged by great change that is coming to the world; a future that is being challenged by those races in the universe who are interfering in human affairs, seeking to take advantage of a weak and divided humanity.

You have come to a point where the future and fate of humanity will be decided in the years to come, and it will be determined by how humanity responds to the great change that is coming to the world and to competition from the universe around you over who will have the commanding influence over the future and the fate of the human family.

People do not realize they are living at such a monumental turning point, such a pivotal time in humanity's long history. It is not in people's thoughts; it is not in people's conversations. But it is at a deeper level in people's experience.

Many people around the world are feeling a great change coming to the world, and they look at the future with concern and anxiety. They sense the great change that is coming over the horizon, even if they cannot yet speak of it openly, or articulate what they are feeling specifically.

Because of the great change that is coming to the world and humanity's encounter with life within the universe, a New Revelation has been sent from the Creator of all life—a great blessing, a great power, a great Message, a great preparation. It has come in a pure form, in a simple form, given incrementally over a long period of time to one man who was sent into the world to bring a New Message from God to a struggling humanity.

For those who will be the first to encounter this New Revelation, it perhaps will be confusing because it deals so much with the future of humanity and to a lesser degree to humanity's present circumstances and difficulties. But this has always been the nature of the great Revelations, the Revelations brought by the Messengers over the course of human history.

The Revelations have not simply been a response to immediate problems and difficulties, but a preparation for the next great stage of human development and evolution. Indeed, in this case, God's New Revelation speaks of a greater challenge to human freedom and sovereignty in this world, a challenge that is known by so very few.

You do not yet realize what is threatening your well-being. You do not yet realize the power and the strength of Knowledge that God has given you. And you do not yet realize that a New Revelation is in the world, and that you are living at a time of Revelation.

If people were really connected to their deeper experience, they could perhaps discern these things. But that is not the case. So the Revelation comes, but few can hear it. Few can recognize it for what it really is. Few can accept the responsibility of what it would mean for their lives to receive a New Message from God. And few can recognize what is coming over the horizon—the great storms that are building in the future and humanity's vulnerability to those forces and races in your local universe who are here to cast their influence over an unsuspecting humanity.

People are beset by other problems—the problems of the day, the anxieties of the moment. These are very real, of course, in many cases, but they are insignificant compared to what is coming.

God knows that humanity is not responding, is not reading the signs of the world and is not responding to Knowledge, the great endowment. So a New Revelation has been sent here, a Revelation unlike anything that has ever been given to humanity before—to prepare you, all of you, for a future that you are not anticipating and for which you are unprepared.

If humanity really understood its position and its vulnerability, then it would recognize why a New Revelation had to be given. It would see that humanity's previous Revelations, all given by God, cannot prepare it for what it is facing now. It would see that humanity's religions and religious institutions are incapable of preparing humanity for the Great Waves of change—for environmental decline; for the loss of food production in the world; for violent weather and for the growing risk of competition, conflict and war between groups and nations over who will have access to the remaining resources of the world, which are being so rapidly depleted at this time.

No religion nor religious institution as it stands today can prepare humanity for the complexities of life in the universe or what humanity must know to preserve human freedom and sovereignty within this world. Indeed, the world's religions have become fractured even within themselves, contentious with each other and anchored in the distant past.

Even the notions and the beliefs about God and Creation are lost in antiquity, are based upon ancient ideas that do not keep pace with the revelations about the expanse of the universe or the great diversity of life that lives around the world and beyond the world.

That is why humanity must now prepare for a new reality, a difficult reality but a redeeming reality. For humanity's facing the Great Waves of change and intervention from the Greater Community hold the greatest promise for human unity and cooperation. For in the face of these things, it becomes quite evident that nations will have to join together to preserve the world, to prevent collapse, to preserve human civilization and to learn about the Greater Community of life in which you have always lived, and in which your world has always existed.

It is a new education, it is a greater need and it has the power to unite a divided humanity. It has the power and the strength to overcome longstanding conflicts and animosities. It is that powerful, it is that urgent and it is that strong, if it can be seen clearly and understood.

But at this moment, humanity is not very intelligent. It does not anticipate the future. It does not prepare for the future. It does not make sacrifices in the moment in order to prepare for future eventualities. It cannot see future eventualities. While there are individuals who can recognize these things and who can be prescient, humanity as a whole is dull and ignorant, self-absorbed and unresponsive to a changing world.

That is why God has sent a New Revelation. The Revelation is here to build human intelligence, to expand human awareness and to teach the meaning of religion and spirituality at the level of Knowledge, at the level of the deeper Intelligence that exists within each person and in all sentient life in the universe.

Here instead of having faith in God, you learn to respond to Knowledge. Here instead of establishing fantastic belief systems and defending them against other belief systems, you begin to respond and to follow Knowledge. Here instead of idolizing and worshiping teachers and messengers, you learn how to recognize Knowledge in one another, which is the wisest part of each person.

God does not run the world. God does not manage the climate. God does not have to take care of every little thing because God has set everything in motion and has given you Knowledge to guide you, to protect you and to prepare you for a greater life of service in the world.

The Lord of all the universes is not preoccupied with your daily affairs, but at the same time has given you a deeper connection so that the Will and the Power of God can speak to you and guide you and give you certainty in the face of calamity or upheaval.

God is so close to you and yet so vast and magnificent and incomprehensible. Your connection to God is at the very center of your Being, but you live your life at the surface of the mind, held there by your fascination and fear of the world, held there by your own fears and obsessions. God is so very close, but God seems so very far away.

Great stories have been told about the Messengers of the past, but who knows the reality of Revelation? Fantastic tales of miracles and superhuman qualities, fantastic tales of cavorting with the Angelic

Host, but who in the world knows what real Revelation looks like, how it is experienced and expressed?

For it has been a very long time since humanity has received a New Revelation from the Creator of all life, and no one living in the world today can account for it. You only have stories from the past. So when a real Revelation occurs, people do not see it. They do not recognize it. They are unresponsive. If they encounter it directly, they doubt it, "How can it be?"

[At first] even the Messenger himself will not proclaim. It is the Message itself that proclaims. The Message proclaims itself to be what it is. It represents its Source and its purpose. It speaks of living fully in the moment and preparing wisely for the future. For the Creator of all life wills that humanity will prepare for its future—a future unlike the past, a future that people will not or cannot see, but which can be seen and felt and known.

This is a calling to you to respond. This is a Message for you about your life and circumstances. This is a Revelation about the real nature of your spirituality and its Source. This is a new understanding about human intelligence and human responsibility. This is a calling for human unity and cooperation. This is a Revelation of what is coming over the horizon and what humanity must do to prepare both collectively and individually. This speaks of the source and center of power within the individual, and where inner freedom can be established and what real freedom means, how it can be preserved and what threatens it today and tomorrow.

Never has such a Teaching been given to humanity before, for the previous Revelations were given to peoples who were illiterate and had no sophistication. In contrast, the New Revelation today is expansive and detailed. It is rich. Its Teaching covers so many subjects. It is the largest Teaching ever given to humanity, for it is being given to a humanity that is now literate and that has a world awareness. Even the nature of Revelation has changed dramatically to meet the growing and changing needs of humanity.

But people's ideas are still lost in the past. They do not understand what Revelation means. They do not recognize it when it appears. They do not see the blessings and the responsibility of living in a time of Revelation. They do not even see the need for a New Revelation.

Nonetheless, a New Message from God has been sent. It is necessary now, for humanity cannot see what is coming. It is unprepared and does not realize the need to prepare. It is living with a misunderstanding of its circumstances, and it cannot see the fruits of its actions or the future consequences of humanity's impact upon the natural world.

Technology has become your new religion, your new god that will save you from everything, or so you think. But your technology cannot prepare you for the Great Waves of change, and it cannot prepare you for your encounter with difficult forces from the universe. Humanity knows not of its strength or its weakness. It is because of this that it is so vulnerable now.

The world has been so depleted, and is being so depleted even at this moment, that the future sustenance and stability for humanity is now imperiled. You must see this and feel this to recognize why a New Revelation would be given. You must have the courage and objectivity to face these things without blame and condemnation upon others. For everyone has created this, and everyone is facing the consequences.

Your future and your destiny will be determined within the next decades. It will be determined now. It will be determined by humanity's wisdom or by its ignorance. That is the choice. That is the decision. That is the great responsibility of your time. That is the great calling of your life.

That is why the New Revelation must speak of humanity's core strength and the power of Knowledge within the individual. For humanity must know where its strength can be found, where its wisdom resides and where it will gain the certainty and the commitment to do what is necessary to preserve human civilization and to thwart intervention from beyond.

These things are unknown to people, but life is moving and the world is changing. Humanity's isolation in the universe is over now, and it will never have it again. The world has changed, but people have not changed with it sufficiently.

There are many new things that must be learned and understood. There are many things that were never needed before that are needed now. There is a great need to uplift the human spirit and to educate humanity about the reality and the spirituality of life in the universe.

But who can teach you these things? They cannot be learned at any university, or in any church or mosque or temple. These things must come from God, for only God knows fully the human heart and the human spirit. Only God knows fully the history and the destiny of humanity.

Thus, a Revelation has been sent, sent through one man, the Messenger. Sent as Messages have always been sent, entering the world in a simple, humble form without pageantry, without great drama, without a great demonstration.

God has given an answer to the prayers and the earnest requests from people from all walks of life, nations and cultures. Your prayers have been answered now, for a New Revelation is in the world. It is your challenge now to find this and to learn of this and to allow it to teach you about the meaning of your life in the world, about what you are preparing for now and the great promise and the great risk that are before the human family.

In the face of these great trials, humanity will have the opportunity to build a new foundation in the world—to unite humanity meaningfully without repression, to act together instead of struggling in Separation from one another, to become mature and wise, to build your strength and to escape the tragedy of the past.

It is the great challenges that will enable you to do this. The very thing that could destroy human civilization is the very thing that could strengthen it and give it a new foundation and a new direction. The adversity you face is redeeming in this regard alone. But do not underestimate the great risk. Do not underestimate the challenge that is facing not only leaders of nations, but every citizen.

So the decision is cast before you: Will you unite and cooperate for the preservation of the world and to meet the great challenge of emerging into a Greater Community of life, or will you fight and struggle over who has access to the remaining resources, ignoring the peril that exists from beyond the world, a peril that will only take advantage of human conflict and human disability?

That is the question, you see. That is the question that is more important and more significant than any other question you could consider at this time, a question that surpasses all of your other concerns. Yet it is a question that is present in so few minds today.

Humanity is unaware of its great strength, and it is unaware of its great perils. It is these two things that have brought a New Message from God into the world for the protection and the advancement of humanity. God seeks to protect human civilization and to give it new life, a new purpose and a new direction, to warn you of the great adversities you face now that are greater than anything your ancestors ever had to deal with.

Therefore, so much depends on human response—human responsibility, the ability to respond. So much depends upon your awareness and decisions, and your ability to recognize you are living in a time of Revelation, in a time of transition into a more difficult and more hazardous world.

So much depends upon human intelligence, the intelligence of individuals who can respond to a New Revelation and can share its wisdom and its guidance with others. So much depends upon the power and the presence of Knowledge within each individual, a power and a presence that is so unknown and that it is not heeded by most.

You have to love humanity and have great faith in humanity to believe that humanity will make the right decisions and follow the path that will provide a new way forward. You have to love humanity and have faith in the spirit of humanity and in the promise and the talents of humanity despite its tragic and prolonged mistakes.

Do not think another race in the universe will come to save you, for those that claim to do so are only here to take advantage of your weakness and your naiveté. Do not think that if human civilization fails, something better or greater can be established as a consequence. Do not underestimate the power of the time in which you live and the great adversities that you now face that still remain unknown to so many.

Do not lose faith in the power and presence of Knowledge within you and within others to recognize and to respond to this and to see the great opportunity to forge a new union in the human family—a union built by necessity, a union built in the fire of necessity, a union built by the recognition that together you can succeed, where in the past you have failed.

The warning is upon you, but the blessing is upon you as well. For God loves humanity and does not want to see you fail or lose your freedom as you emerge into a Greater Community of life in the universe.

You must have this love and this faith and this commitment to humanity as well. If you do, you will begin to experience the power and the grace of Knowledge within yourself. You will see that you too have come into the world at this time specifically to make a unique contribution to certain people in certain circumstances. And though you may not yet realize who these people are or what these circumstances are, you will feel the power and presence of Knowledge moving you, freeing you, reshaping your life, recasting your commitments, moving you in a new direction.

May this blessing be yours to experience, for it is a blessing truly. May these times arouse a newer, deeper commitment and a deeper courage. May you see that your future is before you to be decided at this time of great transition. May you recognize that you as an individual must make these decisions and not simply rely upon others to make them for you. May you recognize that the power and the grace of Knowledge live within you, beneath the surface of your mind.

Within your heart, you know things the mind cannot understand, and that your true identity exists beyond the realm and the reach of the intellect, in the power and the presence of Knowledge.

May you hear these words with your heart with an open mind to see the great love that they demonstrate and the great respect and trust that they offer to you, who do not yet have your own self-respect and trust.

May God's New Revelation illuminate your life and give you strength and courage to navigate the difficult times ahead, and to speak as one voice in this world, and to forge the foundation for a greater future for the human family.

IMPORTANT TERMS

*T*he New Message from God reveals that our world stands at the greatest threshold in the history and evolution of humanity. At this threshold, God has spoken again, revealing the great change that is coming to the world and our destiny within the Greater Community of life beyond our world, for which we are unaware and unprepared.

Here the Revelation redefines certain familiar terms, but within a greater context and introduces other terms that are new to the human family. It is important to understand these terms when reading the texts of the New Message and hearing the Voice of Revelation.

GOD is revealed in the New Message as the Source and Creator of all life and of countless races in the universe. Here the Greater Reality of God is unveiled in the expanded context of life in this world and all life in the universe. This greater context redefines the meaning of our understanding of God and of God's Power and Presence in our lives. The New Message states that to understand what God is doing in our world, we must understand what God is doing in the entire universe. This is now being revealed for the first time through a New Message from God. In the New Message, God is not a divine entity, personage or a singular awareness, but instead a pervasive force and presence that permeates all life and is moving all life in the universe towards a state of unity. God speaks to the deepest part of each person through the power of Knowledge that lives within them.

THE SEPARATION is the ongoing state and condition of being separate from God. The Separation began when part of Creation willed to have the freedom to be apart from God, to live in a state of

Separation. As a result, God created our evolving world and the expanding universe as a place for the separated to live in countless forms and places. Before the Separation, all life was in a timeless state of pure union. It is to this original state of union with God that all those living in Separation are ultimately called to return—through relationship, service and the discovery of Knowledge. It is God's Mission in our world and throughout the universe to reclaim the separated through Knowledge, which is the part of each individual still connected to God.

KNOWLEDGE is the deeper spiritual Intelligence within each person, waiting to be discovered. Knowledge represents the eternal part of us that has never left God. The New Message speaks of Knowledge as the great hope for humanity, an inner power at the heart of each person that God's New Message is here to reveal and to call forth. This deeper spiritual Intelligence exists beyond our thinking mind and the boundaries of our intellect. It alone has the power to guide each of us to our higher purpose and destined relationships in life. The New Message teaches extensively about the reality and experience of Knowledge.

THE ANGELIC ASSEMBLY is the presence of God's Angels who have been assigned to watch over our world and the evolution of humanity. This Assembly is part of the hierarchy established by God to support the redemption and return of all those living in Separation in the physical reality. Every world where sentient life exists is watched over by an Angelic Assembly. The Assembly overseeing our world is now translating the Will of God for our time into human language and understanding, which is now being revealed through the New Message from God. The term Angelic Assembly is synonymous with the terms Angelic Presence and Angelic Host in the text of the New Message.

THE NEW MESSAGE FROM GOD is a communication from God to people of all nations and religions. It represents the next stage of God's progressive Revelation for the human family and comes in response to the great challenges and needs of humanity today. The New Message is over 9000 pages in length and is the largest Revelation ever given to the world, given now to a literate world of global communication and growing global awareness. The New Message is not an offshoot or reformation of any past tradition and is not given for one tribe, nation or group alone. It is God's New Message for the whole world, which is now facing Great Waves of environmental, social and political change and the new threshold of emerging into a Greater Community of intelligent life in the universe.

THE VOICE OF REVELATION is the united voice of the Angelic Assembly delivering God's Message through a Messenger sent into the world for this task. Here the Assembly speaks as one Voice, the many speaking as one. For the first time in history, you are able to hear the actual Voice of Revelation speaking through God's Messenger. It is this Voice that has spoken to all God's Messengers in the past. The Word and the Sound of the Voice of Revelation are in the world and are available for you to hear in their original audio form.

THE MESSENGER is the one chosen, prepared and sent into the world by the Angelic Assembly to receive the New Message from God. The Messenger for this time is Marshall Vian Summers. Marshall is a humble man with no position in the world who has undergone a long and difficult preparation to receive God's New Revelation and bring it to the world. He is charged with the great burden, blessing and responsibility of presenting this Revelation to a divided and conflicted world. He is the first of God's Messengers to reveal the reality of a Greater Community of intelligent life in the universe. The Messenger has been engaged in this process of Revelation since the year 1982.

THE PRESENCE refers to different but interconnected realities: the presence of Knowledge within the individual, the Presence of the Angelic Assembly that oversees the world or ultimately the Presence of God in the universe. The Presence of these three realities offers a life-changing experience of grace and relationship. All three are connected to the larger process of growth and redemption for us, for the world and for the universe at large. Together they represent the mystery and purpose of our lives, which the New Message reveals to us in the clearest possible terms. The New Revelation offers a modern pathway for experiencing the power of the Presence in your life.

STEPS TO KNOWLEDGE is an ancient book of spiritual practice now being given by God to the world for the first time. Steps provides the lessons and practices necessary for learning and living the New Message from God. In beginning the Steps, you embark on a journey of discovering Knowledge, the mysterious source of your inner power and authority, and with it the essential relationships you are destined to find. Its 365 daily "steps," or practices, lead you to a personal revelation about your life and destiny. In taking this greater journey, you can discover the power of Knowledge and your experience of profound inner knowing, which lead you to your higher purpose and calling in life.

THE GREATER COMMUNITY is the larger universe of intelligent life in which our world has always existed. This Greater Community encompasses all worlds in the universe where sentient life exists, in all states of evolution and development. The New Message reveals that humanity is in an early and adolescent phase of its development and that the time has now come for humanity's emergence into the Greater Community. It is here, standing at the threshold of space, that humanity discovers that it is not alone in the universe, or even within its own world.

THE GREATER COMMUNITY WAY OF KNOWLEDGE is a timeless tradition representing God's work in the universe to reclaim the separated in all worlds through the power of Knowledge that is inherent in all intelligent life. To understand what God is doing in our world, we must begin to understand what God is doing in the entire universe. For the first time in history, The Greater Community Way of Knowledge is being presented to the world through a New Message from God. The New Message opens the portal to this timeless work of God underway throughout the universe in which we live. We stand at the threshold of emerging into this Greater Community and must now have access to The Greater Community Way of Knowledge in order to understand our destiny as a race and successfully navigate the challenges of interacting with life in the universe.

THE INTERVENTION is a dangerous form of contact underway by certain races from the Greater Community who are here to take advantage of a weak and divided humanity. This is occurring at a time when the human family is entering a period of increasing breakdown and disorder, in the face of the Great Waves of change. The Intervention presents itself as a benign and redeeming force while in reality its ultimate goal is to undermine human freedom and self-determination and take control of the world and its resources. The New Message reveals that the Intervention seeks to secretly establish its influence here in the minds and hearts of people at a time of growing confusion, conflict and vulnerability. God is calling us, as the native peoples of this world, to oppose this Intervention, to alert and educate others and to put forth our own rules of engagement as an emerging race. Our response to the Intervention and the Greater Community at large is the one thing that can unite a fractured and divided human family at a time of the greatest need and consequence for our race.

THE GREAT WAVES OF CHANGE are a set of powerful environmental, economic and social forces now converging in the world. The Great Waves are the result of humanity's misuse and overuse of the world, its resources and its environment. The Great Waves have the power to drastically alter the face of the world—producing economic instability, runaway climate change, violent weather and the loss of arable land and freshwater, threatening to produce a world condition of great difficulty and human suffering. The Great Waves are not an end times or apocalyptic event, but instead a challenging period of transition to a new world reality. The New Message reveals what is coming for the world and provides a preparation to enable us to navigate a radically changing world. God is calling for human unity and cooperation born now out of sheer necessity for the preservation and protection of human civilization. Together with the Intervention, the Great Waves represents one of the two great threats facing humanity and a major reason why God has spoken again.

HIGHER PURPOSE refers to the specific contribution each person was sent into the world to make and the unique relationships that will enable the fulfillment of this purpose. Knowledge within the individual holds their higher purpose and destiny for them, which cannot be ascertained by the intellect alone. These must be discovered, followed and expressed in service to others to be fully realized. The world needs the demonstration of this higher purpose from many more people as never before.

SPIRITUAL FAMILY refers to the small working groups formed after the Separation to enable all individuals to work towards greater states of union and relationship, undertaking this over a long span of time, culminating in their final return to God. Your Spiritual Family represents the relationships you have reclaimed through Knowledge during your long journey through Separation. Some members of your Spiritual Family are in the world and some are beyond the world. The Spiritual Families are a part of the mysterious Plan of God to free and reunite all those living in Separation.

ANCIENT HOME refers to the reality of life and the state of awareness and relationship you had before entering the world, and to which you will return after your life in the world. Your Ancient Home is a timeless state of connection and relationship with your Spiritual Family, The Assembly and God.

The Story of the Messenger

Marshall Vian Summers is the Messenger for the New Message from God. For over three decades he has been the recipient of a Divine Revelation given to prepare humanity for the great environmental, social and economic changes that are coming to the world and for humanity's contact with intelligent life in the universe.

In 1982, at the age of 33, Marshall Vian Summers was called into the deserts of the American Southwest where he had a direct encounter with the Angelic Presence, who had been guiding and preparing him for his future role and calling. This encounter forever altered the course of his life and initiated him into a deeper relationship with the Angelic Assembly, requiring that he surrender his life to God. This began the long, mysterious process of receiving God's New Message for humanity.

Following this mysterious initiation, he received the first revelations of the New Message from God. Over the decades since, a vast Revelation for humanity has unfolded, at times slowly and at times in great torrents. During these long years, he had to proceed with the support of only a few individuals, not knowing what this growing Revelation would mean and where it would ultimately lead.

The Messenger has walked a long and difficult road to receive and present the largest Revelation ever given to the human family. Still today the Voice of Revelation continues to speak through him as he faces the great challenge of bringing God's New Revelation to a troubled and conflicted world.

Read more about the life and story of the Messenger
Marshall Vian Summers:
www.newmessage.org/story-of-marshall-vian-summers

Read and hear the original revelation *The Story of the Messenger:*
www.newmessage.org/story-of-the-messenger

Hear and watch the world teachings of the Messenger:
www.newmessage.org/messenger

THE VOICE OF REVELATION

For the first time in history, you can hear the Voice of Revelation, such a Voice as spoke to the prophets and Messengers of the past and is now speaking again through a new Messenger who is in the world today.

The Voice of Revelation is not the voice of one individual, but that of the entire Angelic Assembly speaking together, all as one. Here God communicates beyond words to the Angelic Assembly, who then translate God's Message into human words and language that we can comprehend.

The revelations of this book were originally spoken in this manner by the Voice of Revelation through the Messenger Marshall Vian Summers. This process of Divine Revelation has occurred since 1982. The Revelation continues to this day.

Hear the original audio recordings of the
Voice of Revelation, which is the Source of the text contained
in this book and throughout the New Message:
www.newmessage.org/experience

Learn more about the Voice of Revelation,
what it is and how it speaks through the Messenger:
www.newmessage.org/voiceofrevelation

About The Society for the New Message from God

Founded in 1992 by Marshall Vian Summers, The Society for the New Message from God is an independent religious 501(c)(3) non-profit organization that is primarily supported by readers and students of the New Message, receiving no sponsorship or revenue from any government or religious organization.

The Society's mission is to bring the New Message from God to people everywhere so that humanity can find its common ground, preserve the Earth, protect human freedom and advance human civilization as we stand at the threshold of great change and a universe full of intelligent life.

Marshall Vian Summers and The Society have been given the immense responsibility of bringing the New Message into the world. The members of The Society are a small group of dedicated individuals who have committed themselves to fulfill this mission. For them, it is both a burden and a great blessing to give themselves wholeheartedly in this great service to humanity.

The Society for the New Message

Contact us:

P.O. Box 1724 Boulder, CO 80306-1724
(303) 938-8401 (800) 938-3891
011 303 938 84 01 (International)
(303) 938-1214 (fax)
society@newmessage.org
www.newmessage.org
www.marshallsummers.com
www.alliesofhumanity.org
www.newknowledgelibrary.org

Connect with us:

www.youtube.com/thenewmessagefromgod
www.facebook.com/newmessagefromgod
www.facebook.com/marshallsummers
www.twitter.com/godsnewmessage

Donate to support The Society and join a community of givers who are helping bring the New Message to the world:
www.newmessage.org/donate

ABOUT THE WORLDWIDE COMMUNITY OF THE NEW MESSAGE FROM GOD

The New Message from God is being studied and practiced by people around the world. Representing more than 90 countries and studying the New Message in over 30 languages, a worldwide community of students has formed to both receive the New Message and support the Messenger in bringing God's New Message to the world.

The New Message has the power to awaken the sleeping brilliance in people everywhere and bring new inspiration and wisdom into the lives of people from all nations and faith traditions.

Learn more about the worldwide community of people who are learning and living the New Message and taking the Steps to Knowledge in their lives.

Read and hear the original Revelation *The Worldwide Community of God's New Message:*
www.newmessage.org/theworldwidecommunity

Join the free Worldwide Community site where you can meet other students and engage with the Messenger:
www.community.newmessage.org

Learn more about the educational opportunities available in the Worldwide Community:

Community Site - www.community.newmessage.org/
New Message Free School - www.community.newmessage.org/school
Live Internet Broadcasts and International Events -
www.newmessage.org/events

Encampment - www.newmessage.org/encampment
Online Library of Text and Audio -
www.newmessage.org/experience

Books of the New Message from God

God Has Spoken Again

The One God

The New Messenger

The Greater Community

The Journey to a New Life

The Power of Knowledge

Steps to Knowledge

Greater Community Spirituality

The Great Waves of Change

Life in the Universe

Wisdom from the Greater Community I & II

Secrets of Heaven

Relationships & Higher Purpose

Living The Way of Knowledge